Ravenscourt

B·O·O·K·S

Teacher's Guide

Overcoming Adversity

Books 1–8

The Last Boat

No Need to Shout

*Playing Through Pain:
The Story of Roberto Clemente*

Once There Were Two

Walls of Water

Robinson Crusoe's Adventures

The Trojan War

Monte Cristo's Prison Years

Cathy L. Watkins, Ph.D., Consultant

Columbus, OH • Chicago, IL • Redmond, WA

The **McGraw-Hill** Companies

Table of Contents

SRAonline.com

 SRA

Copyright © 2004 by SRA/McGraw-Hill.

All rights reserved. Except as permitted under the United States Copyright Act, no part of this publication may be reproduced or distributed in any form or by any means, or stored in a database or retrieval system, without the prior written permission of the publisher, unless otherwise indicated.

Send all inquiries to:
SRA/McGraw-Hill
8787 Orion Place
Columbus, OH 43240-4027

Printed in the United States of America.

ISBN 0-07-601663-3

4 5 6 7 8 9 MAL 07 06 05 04

Placing Students

Written for middle school to young adult readers, **Ravenscourt Books** provides research-based strategies for enhancing the comprehension and fluency of struggling readers. Each of these engaging fiction and nonfiction titles is

- tailored to students' independent reading levels to encourage struggling readers to read more.

- designed to provide frequent opportunities for reading to improve fluency and overall reading achievement.
- carefully aligned to **Corrective Reading** to prevent frustration and to build success.

Use the chart below to place your students in the appropriate set of **Ravenscourt Books.**

	The Unexpected	Overcoming Adversity	Reaching Goals
For students who have completed	*Corrective Reading Decoding B1**	*Corrective Reading Decoding B2**	*Corrective Reading Decoding C** lesson 60
Reading Level	2	3	5
Decodability	> 97%	> 95%	> 95%

Or have attained comparable skills

Components

The **Using Ravenscourt Books** section explains how to incorporate these components into an effective supplemental reading program.

Chapter Books
- include eight age-appropriate books in each set.
- feature a variety of genres—retold classics, fiction, and nonfiction.
- practice vocabulary and decoding skills found in **Corrective Reading.**
- provide fast-moving story lines for independent reading.

Fluency Audiotapes/CDs
- model correct pronunciation, phrasing, intonation, and expression.
- assist students in improving their oral-reading fluency.

Evaluation and Tracking Software
- motivate students with immediate feedback on quizzes.
- score, record, and track student progress automatically.

Teacher's Guides
- outline ways to use the series in your classroom.
- include comprehension activities, word lists, and fluency practice.
- provide prereading activities and postreading writing activities.
- address reading and language arts standards.

Online Support

Go to **SRAonline** and click on **Ravenscourt Books** for additional support and materials such as

- additional lesson plans.
- extra essay questions.
- family letters in Spanish and English.
- fluency information and research.
- readability and decodability information.
- scope and sequence including decoding and reading skills, literary terms, and types of writing.

Reading and Fluency

Reading

Reading is not simply decoding or word recognition; it is understanding the text. Students who read slowly or hesitantly are not able to concentrate on meaning.

Fluency

Fluency bridges the gap between decoding and comprehension and characterizes proficient reading. Increased oral-reading fluency improves reading comprehension

Fluent and Nonfluent Readers

The chart below is an easy way to compare fluent and nonfluent readers. If students have several of the listed characteristics of nonfluent readers, then refer to the sections on Assessing Fluency and Fluency Practice in the **Using *Ravenscourt Books*** section on the following pages.

A Fluent Reader	A Nonfluent Reader
Reads words accurately	Reads with omissions, pauses, mispronunciations, insertions, and substitutions, and reverses word order
Decodes automatically	Reads word-by-word, focusing on words
Reads smoothly	Reads haltingly
Reads rapidly at an appropriate rate	Reads slowly, hesitantly
Reads with expression and phrasing	Reads without expression; ignores punctuation
Reads with understanding of text	Reads with limited comprehension
Reads so text sounds like speech	Reads without natural intonation

Oral-Reading Fluency

Oral-reading fluency is the ability to read accurately, at an appropriate rate, and with good expression and phrasing. The foundation for oral reading fluency is automatic word recognition and extensive practice with materials that are easy for the students to read.

Oral-reading fluency develops as a result of multiple opportunities to practice reading successfully. The primary strategy for developing reading fluency is to provide extensive and frequent opportunities for students to read text with high levels of accuracy. This means that selected passages should be ones that the students are able to read with at least 95% accuracy.

Repeated and monitored oral reading is an effective intervention strategy for students who do not read fluently. By reading the same passage a number of times, students become familiar with the words it contains and recognize them automatically. This improves reading fluency and overall reading achievement. It also builds confidence and motivation—particularly when students chart their progress.

The minimum target oral-fluency rate is 100 *words read correctly per minute* (wcpm) for **The Unexpected,** 120 wcpm for **Overcoming Adversity,** and 150 wcpm for **Reaching Goals.**

How to assess fluency, how to set realistic target rates, and how to practice fluency will be discussed in greater detail in the **Using *Ravenscourt Books*** section.

Grouping

Students who have completed *Decoding B2* will have mastered the decoding skills and vocabulary necessary to read independently the stories in **Overcoming Adversity**.

Ravenscourt Books may be taught to the whole class, small groups, or pairs, or may be used for individual student reading. Assign each student to a partner. The partners will read the same story at the same time. Partners can do paired readings for fluency practice.

Scheduling

Ravenscourt Books is a supplement to *Corrective Reading* and should be scheduled in addition to the regular lessons. Times to use the books include

- reading and language arts block,
- before- and after-school programs,
- intersession classes,
- summer school,
- or out-of-school reading with parental support.

A Suggested Lesson Plan for *Ravenscourt Books*

Day 1	1) Help students select a book, and introduce the series. 2) Assess students' initial oral-reading fluency. (See Assessing Fluency on page 4.) 3) Help students complete the **Building Background** activities.
Day 2	1) Teacher preteaches unfamiliar words for the first chapter (found in the **Word Lists** section of the *Teacher's Guide* for each book). 2) Students listen to a fluent reader read the first chapter, following along with the text. 3) Student pairs take turns reading the chapter again. 4) Students take the **Chapter Quiz.** 5) Some students will do repeated readings to improve oral-reading fluency.
Days 3–7	Repeat the procedure for Day 2 for the subsequent chapters.
Day 8	1) Students complete **Thinking and Writing** section. 2) Teacher takes fluency scores using one of the **Fluency Passages** for the book. Students enter scores on graph. 2) Teacher may assign a **Book Report Form** to be completed on a blackline master or on the *Evaluation and Tracking Software.*

Selecting Books

The books in each set are leveled so that students can start with any book in the set. However, students generally find contemporary fiction easier to read than nonfiction and retold classics.

On pages 13–14 you will find **Book Summaries** that give a brief outline of each book.

- If the book is a retold classic, information about the original *author* is included.

- If a book is a good tool for teaching a *literary term*, the term is explained. The teacher should teach the term before the students begin reading.

- The last section includes *other resources*—books, films, or Web sites—that contain related information. These resources can be used for extra credit, reports, projects, and so on.

Using *Ravenscourt Books*

Introducing the Series

1. Write the theme—**The Unexpected, Overcoming Adversity,** or **Reaching Goals**—on the board.
   - Tell the students that the books in each set all relate in some way to this common idea or theme.
   - Brainstorm ideas about the theme, and write the students' ideas on a large sheet of chart paper. Include words, topics, and types of stories that are related to the theme. Post this list for student reference.

2. The books in each set represent several genres—fiction, nonfiction, biography, science fiction, historical fiction, retold classics, humor, and so on.
   - Ask the students to read the title and the summary on the back of the book they chose.
   - Have the students predict how that book relates to the theme.
   - If the book is nonfiction, ask the students to predict what kinds of questions it could answer.
   - If the book is fiction, ask students who the story is about and what problems the main characters will face.

Whole-Class Instruction

The following suggestions are designed for whole-class instruction but may be modified for small groups or individual instruction.

Set up classes in the *Evaluation and Tracking Software* or make a copy of the **Individual Progress Chart** for each student.

Assessing Fluency

Make a class set of copies of the **Fluency Graph** on page 9 of the *Teacher's Guide.* Follow these steps to ASSESS STUDENTS' INITIAL ORAL-READING FLUENCY.

1. Select a passage of the appropriate length (100–150 words) that is at the student's instructional reading level (95% accuracy).

- Use the **Fluency Passage** found on page 24 of the *Teacher's Guide.*

2. Ask the student to do a one-minute reading of the unrehearsed passage.

3. Ask the student whether she/he is ready.
   - Then say: **Please begin.**

4. Follow along as the student reads.
   - When an error occurs, tell the student the word that was missed and mark the error.
   - Count the following as errors: mispronunciations, omissions, substitutions, insertions, and failure to identify a word within three seconds.
   - Don't mark words that the student self-corrects. Don't mark off for proper nouns.

5. At the end of one minute, make a vertical line on the page after the last word read.

6. Count the number of words up to the last word read.

7. Subtract the number of errors to determine the number of *words read correctly per minute* (wcpm).

8. Enter the number of words read correctly on the **Fluency Graph** on page 9 by filling in the column to the appropriate number with a red pencil.

9. Circle the number of errors made at the bottom of the graph.

10. Review any words that the student missed and provide practice on those words. The minimum goals for fluency are the following:

- The goal for students who have completed *Decoding B1* or have equivalent skills is to read the books in **The Unexpected** at a minimum rate of 100 words read correctly per minute (wcpm).
- The goal for students who have completed *Decoding B2* is to read **Overcoming Adversity** books at a minimum of 120 wcpm.
- The goal for students who have completed lesson 60 of *Decoding C* is to read **Reaching Goals** books at a minimum of 150 wcpm.

Building Background

Use the **Building Background** section in the *Teacher's Guide* or on the *Evaluation and Tracking Software.* Here are two ways to use this section as a whole-class activity. Preteach the section using this activity.

1. Divide the students into small groups. Hand out copies of the **Building Background** page for that book.

2. Read the first question in the *What You Know* section.

   • Use a timer, and tell the students: **You have three minutes to brainstorm this question. Begin.**

   • When time is up, have the groups share their ideas. Write key words and phrases on the board.

   • Set a timer, and tell the students: **You have two minutes to write a short answer to this question. Put down your pencils when you finish.**

   • When time is up, follow the same procedure with the next question. Suggested answers are found in the **Answer Keys** for each book.

3. As you read the words in the box in the *There's a Word for It* section, ask: **What does (word) mean?** (Call on individual students.)

   • Write correct synonyms or definitions on the board. Refer students to other resources as needed.

   • When the students have defined all the words, read the first sentence aloud and say: **Which word fits best in this sentence?** (Call on individual students. Use prompts from the board as needed.)

   • Follow this procedure for all of the words.

4. Collect the papers and score them based on the number of correct answers. Refer to the **Answer Keys.**

This section may also be used as a pretest.

1. Hand out copies of the **Building Background** page. Have students take turns reading the questions in the *What You Know* section.

   • Set a timer and tell the students: **You have ten minutes to answer these questions. Write your answers in pencil. Put down your pencils when you finish.**

2. Have students read the words in the box in the *There's a Word for It* section.

   • Set a timer and tell the students: **You have five minutes to write the correct words in the sentences. Put down your pencils when you finish.**

   • When time is up, collect the papers and score them based on completion and effort. Refer to the **Answer Keys** for each book.

3. Return the papers and have students share their answers. Students should write corrections in pen on their papers.

The teacher may enter the scores on the **Individual Progress Chart** found in the *Teacher's Guide* or on the *Evaluation and Tracking Software.*

Word List

Follow this procedure to preteach the words for each chapter of every book.

1. Provide students with a copy of the **Word List** page or copy the words on the board. Underline word parts if appropriate. Begin by saying:

   • **These are the proper nouns in Chapter 1. Proper Nouns are words that name a particular person, place, or thing. What are proper nouns?** (Signal.) *Words that name a particular person, place, or thing.*

2. **Touch the first word in the column.**

   • Point to an underlined word part and say: **What sound?** (Signal.)

   • **What word?** (Signal.)

   • (Repeat until firm.)

3. For difficult and irregular words, say: **Touch the first word in the column.**

   • **The word is _____.** (Signal.)

   • **What word?** (Signal.)

   • **Spell _____.** (Signal for each letter.)

   • **What word?** (Signal.)

   • (Repeat until firm.)

4. Follow the same procedures with *There's a Word for It, Word Families,* and *Unfamiliar Words*. Discuss the meanings of the words. Use the words in sentences as needed.

   * Then point to each word, say the word, and say: **What does (word) mean?** (Call on individual students.)

   * (Repeat until firm.)

5. In *Word Families,* once the students know the meaning of the words, establish the relationships among the words.

   * Have the students use the words in simple sentences.

   * Indicate which form of the word is the base and how affixes change the base.

Another way to use the **Word Lists** is to provide the students with copies of the page and have them listen to the words pronounced on the *Fluency Audiotapes* or *CDs*.

Reading the Chapter

First the student listens to a fluent reader read the chapter. The fluency model may be the teacher, a parent, a tutor, a teacher's aide, a peer, or the *Fluency Audiotapes* or *CDs*. The student reads along, tracking the text with his or her finger.

Next students take turns reading the chapter with their peer partner. An individual student reads aloud to the teacher, tutor, or parent who gives feedback, points out missed words, and models using punctuation to improve expressive reading.

Chapter Quiz

After the second reading of the chapter, the student takes the **Chapter Quiz.** The quizzes have multiple-choice, true or false, or sequence questions. The chapter quizzes are available on the computer version or as blackline masters in the *Teacher's Guide.* Use the **Answer Key** to score the blackline masters and enter scores on the **Individual Progress Chart** found on page 8. The *Evaluation and Tracking Software* will automatically grade and record the scores for each **Chapter Quiz.**

Students should take each quiz once and do their best the first time. Students must score a minimum of 80% to continue. If the student does not score 80%, the student should reread the chapter before retaking the quiz.

Fluency Practice

Fluency practice improves comprehension. The teacher may choose different ways to practice fluency, depending on the student's needs. The minimum target rate is 100 wcpm for **The Unexpected,** 120 wcpm for **Overcoming Adversity,** and 150 wcpm for **Reaching Goals.**

For students who are close to the target rate, have the student reread the whole chapter using one of these techniques.

Echo reading A fluent reader reads a sentence, and the student echoes it—repeats it with the same intonation and phrasing.

Unison or choral reading A pair, group, or class reads a chapter aloud together.

Paired reading The student reads a page aloud and receives feedback from his/her peer partner.

Record the fluency scores on the **Fluency Graph** found in the *Teacher's Guide* or on the *Evaluation and Tracking Software.* Recording progress motivates student achievement and records student practices as well as progress.

For students who are significantly below the target rate, conduct **REPEATED READINGS TO IMPROVE ORAL-READING FLUENCY.** The student will reread the passages marked by asterisks in each of the books' chapters.

1. Set a target rate for the passage.

   * The target rate should be high enough to require the student to reread the passage several times.

   * A reasonable target rate is 40% higher than the baseline level.

   * For example, if the student initially reads the passage at a rate of 60 words correct per minute, the target rate for that passage would be 84 wcpm (**60 x .40 = 24; 60 + 24 = 84).**

2. Have the student listen to the passage read fluently by a skilled reader or the corresponding *Fluency Audiotape* or *CD* while following along by pointing to the words as they are read.

3. After listening to the fluency model, the student rereads the same passage aloud for one minute.

   - A partner listens and records errors but does not interrupt the reader during the one-minute timed reading.

   - If the student makes more than six errors, he/she should listen to the fluency model again.

4. The student should read the same passage three to five times during the session or until the target rate is met, whichever comes first.

   - After each rereading, the student records the wcpm on the graph with a blue pencil.

   - If the target rate is not met, have the student read the same passage again the next day.

   - If the target rate is met, the student repeats the procedure with the next chapter.

Thinking and Writing

Many state assessments require students to produce extended writing about a story or an article they have read. Like **Building Background,** this section is not computer-scored and may be used in one of several ways. The *Think About It* section is intended to help students summarize what they have read and to relate the book to other books in the set, to the theme, or to their life experiences.

1. The questions in the *Think About It* section can be used for discussion.

   - Students discuss the questions in small groups and then write their individual responses on the blackline masters or on the computer.

   - The teacher may score the response using a variety of rubrics. For example, the teacher could give points for all reasonable responses in complete sentences that begin with a capital letter and end with punctuation.

2. For certain students, the teacher may ask the questions and prompt the student to give a thoughtful oral response.

3. Another option is to use *Think About It* as a mini-assessment. Have the students answer the questions independently on paper or using the *Evaluation and Tracking Software.*

The *Write About It* section gives students extended practice writing about what they have read. The teacher may use as much of the writing process as time allows.

1. Small groups are each assigned a different question to brainstorm. Allot approximately eight minutes for students to discuss and write on chart paper key ideas and points about the question.

2. Tell the students that they will choose which question they wish to write about, so they need to listen carefully to each group's presentation in order to make up their minds.

   - Have each group tape their papers to the board. The group reports what they discussed, and other class members add comments or ideas.

   - After each question has been discussed, students choose a question to write about.

The students may answer on the blackline master or using the *Evaluation and Tracking Software.* To motivate students, the computer version includes a spelling checker and a variety of fonts and colors for students to choose. This section is teacher-scored. Scores may be entered on a copy of the **Individual Progress Chart** or on the *Evaluation and Tracking Software.*

Students may keep their essays in a writing portfolio. At the end of the term students choose one of their essays to improve, using the writing process.

Book Report Forms

The **Book Report Forms** are a structured, alternative writing experience. There are book report forms for nonfiction, for fiction, and for biography or character analysis. The forms are available as blackline masters or on the *Evaluation and Tracking Software.* Scores may be entered on the blackline master or computer version of the **Individual Progress Chart.**

Individual Progress Chart

Name: _____ **Class:** _____

Book Title	Building Background	Chapter 1 Quiz	Chapter 2 Quiz	Chapter 3 Quiz	Chapter 4 Quiz	Chapter 5 Quiz	Chapter 6 Quiz	Thinking and Writing	Book Report
The Last Boat									
No Need to Shout									
Playing Through Pain: The Story of Roberto Clemente									
Once There Were Two									
Walls of Water									
Robinson Crusoe's Adventures									
The Trojan War									
Monte Cristo's Prison Years									

• Enter the percentage correct score for each quiz or activity. Shaded quizzes will be scored automatically by the *Evaluation and Tracking Software.*

Overcoming Adversity

Fluency Graph

Name: _____   Class: _____

Fluency Graph

Instructions:

1. Read a fluency passage for one minute.   2. Find Column 1.   3. Color the column to the number that shows how far you read.

4. Mark the numbers of errors in the chart at the bottom.

WCPM RATE
Number of Words read correctly in one minute

Date	10	20	30	40	50	60	70	80	90	100	110	120	130	140	150	160	170	180

ERRORS

Above 6

6	5	4	3	2	1	0
6	5	4	3	2	1	0
6	5	4	3	2	1	0
6	5	4	3	2	1	0
6	5	4	3	2	1	0
6	5	4	3	2	1	0
6	5	4	3	2	1	0
6	5	4	3	2	1	0
6	5	4	3	2	1	0
6	5	4	3	2	1	0
6	5	4	3	2	1	0
6	5	4	3	2	1	0
6	5	4	3	2	1	0
6	5	4	3	2	1	0
6	5	4	3	2	1	0
6	5	4	3	2	1	0
6	5	4	3	2	1	0
6	5	4	3	2	1	0
6	5	4	3	2	1	0
6	5	4	3	2	1	0
6	5	4	3	2	1	0
6	5	4	3	2	1	0
6	5	4	3	2	1	0
6	5	4	3	2	1	0
6	5	4	3	2	1	0
6	5	4	3	2	1	0
6	5	4	3	2	1	0
6	5	4	3	2	1	0
6	5	4	3	2	1	0
6	5	4	3	2	1	0
6	5	4	3	2	1	0
6	5	4	3	2	1	0

Book Report Form

Nonfiction Form

Fill in the form below to describe the book you read.

Name:	Title of Book:
Chapter 1:_____ Key Points • • •	**Chapter 2:**_____ Key Points • • •
Chapter 3:_____ Key Points • • •	**Chapter 4:**_____ Key Points • • •
Chapter 5:_____ Key Points • • •	**Chapter 6:**_____ Key Points • • •

Fiction Form

Fill in the form below to describe the book you read.

Name:	Title of Book:
List the main character(s) and his or her important characteristics.	**Setting**—List the places and times that were important to the story.

	Where	When

Describe the theme of this book.

Describe the most important plot event.

What did you like about this book?

Rate this book from 1 to 5 ☆s by circling the stars.

☆　☆　☆　☆　☆

Book Report Form

Name:_____

Biography/Character Description

Describe the main character from your book by writing descriptions in the boxes as needed.

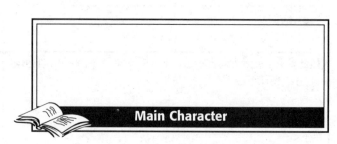
Main Character

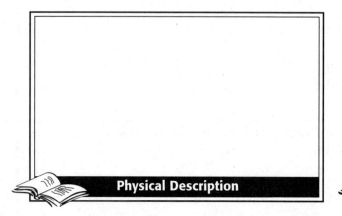
Physical Description

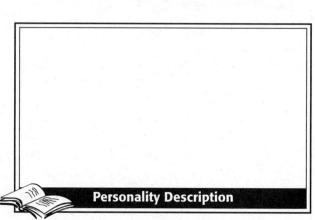
Personality Description

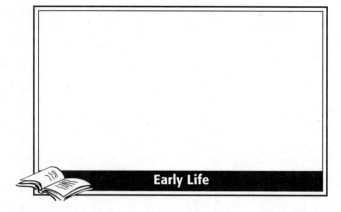
Early Life

Influential People

Achievements

Significant Events

The Last Boat

By Ilie Ruby

Summary

Luis thinks of himself as a loser. When his much-admired older brother is killed, Luis thinks it should have been him instead. When Luis's mother hears him talking about joining the gang, she sends him to stay with an aunt who lives near the ocean. Luis learns about himself as he learns to sail. Even though he finishes last in a race, he discovers that he isn't a loser after all.

Literary Terms

Simile: A comparison using *like* or *as*

Coming-of-age story: The main character is initiated into adulthood through knowledge, experience, or both. Changes may be from ignorance to knowledge, innocence to experience, false view of the world to correct view, idealism to realism, or immature responses to mature responses.

Other Resources

Book: Adkins, Jan. *The Craft of Sail: A Primer of Sailing* (Walker and Company, 1994)

Movies: *Wind* (1992), *White Squall* (1996), *Learn to Sail* (1999)

Web sites: www.ussailing.org/

www.cccturtle.org/kemps.htm

www.mltd.com/travel/turtlehelp.html

No Need to Shout

By Rick Watson

Summary

A childish prank turns into a life-threatening disaster for best friends Jamal and Vernon. Jamal is in a coma, and Vernon has lost his hearing. Fortunately, both boys survive, but Vernon is hiding a guilty secret about his friend. Vernon learns how to cope with his hearing loss, and Jamal, after a long course of physical therapy, recovers. Even though they go through a rough time, their friendship endures, and they learn many valuable lessons.

Literary Terms

Dialogue: The words spoken by characters in a story

Coming-of-age story: The main character is initiated into adulthood through knowledge, experience, or both. Changes may be from ignorance to knowledge, innocence to experience, false view of the world to correct view, idealism to realism, or immature responses to mature responses.

Other Resources

Book: Matlin, Marlee. *Deaf Child Crossing* (Simon & Schuster Books for Young Readers, 2002)

Movie: *Signing Made Easy* (2000)

Web sites:

www.masterstech-home.com/ASLDict.html

www.where.com/scott.net/asl/

Playing Through Pain: The Story of Roberto Clemente

By Barbara Wood

Summary

Roberto Clemente is one of the greatest legends in the history of baseball. Clemente was born to play baseball, and he loved it from the start. Clemente paved the way for other Latino baseball players. He showed courage because he played baseball in spite of poverty, physical injury, chronic health problems, and ethnic prejudice. Sadly, Clemente died at a young age. Clemente is remembered as a great ballplayer and a great humanitarian.

Literary Term

Biography: An account of a person's life written by another person

Other Resources

Books: Dunham, Montrew and Meryl Henderson. *Roberto Clemente: Young Ball Player* (Aladdin Library, 1997); Kingsbury, Robert. *Roberto Clemente* (Rosen Publishing Group, 2003); Wagenheim, Kal and Wilfrid Sheed. *Clemente!* (Olmstead Press, 2001)

Movies: *Roberto Clemente* (1993); *Roberto Clemente—A Video Tribute* (1997) (in Spanish)

Web site: www.robertoclemente21.com/

Once There Were Two

By Carole Gerber

Summary

Major league baseball once had a very different look. It wasn't the uniforms; it was the players. There were no African American players on the field. Segregation kept them in their own league. But what a league it was! Many of baseball's all-time great players played in the Negro Leagues. When Jackie Robinson broke the baseball color barrier in 1947, it was a great step for African Americans. Yet, this was the beginning of the end for the Negro Leagues. Segregation is a part of American history that some would like to forget. But one thing should never be forgotten—the great players of the Negro Leagues.

Literary Term

Nonfiction: A factual piece of literature

Other Resources

Book: McKissack, Patricia, et al. *Black Diamond: The Story of the Negro Baseball Leagues* (Polaris, 1998)

Movies: *Only the Ball Was White* (1993); *The Bingo Long Traveling All-Stars and Motor Kings* (1976); *Soul of the Game* (1996); *Baseball—A Film by Ken Burns* (1994)

Web sites: www.negroleaguebaseball.com/

www.nlbm.com/intro.html

www.nlbpa.com

Book Summaries

Walls of Water

By Susan Blackaby

Summary

In 1889 a dam broke and a wall of water roared into Johnstown, Pennsylvania. More than 100 years later, the Great Flood of 1993 devastated large areas in the Mississippi River Basin. Things had changed in 100 years. In 1889 more than 2,000 people lost their lives. In the Great Flood of 1993 only 48 people died. In the century between the two disasters, flood watchers learned how to predict flooding, to warn people, and to protect property.

Literary Term

Nonfiction: A factual piece of literature

Foreshadowing: An author's hints about events that will occur later in a story

Other Resources

Book: Walker, Paul Robert. *Head for the Hills! The Amazing True Story of the Johnstown Flood* (Random House, 1993)

Movies: *20th Century with Mike Wallace—Underwater: The Great Flood of '93* (1999); *Untamed Earth: Ferocious Floods* (2003); *Johnstown Flood DVD* (2003)

Web site: www.jaha.org/flood/

Robinson Crusoe's Adventures

Retold by Carole Gerber

Summary

As a young man, Crusoe ignored his family when they told him not to go to sea. He soon found himself shipwrecked on a deserted island. Crusoe taught himself how to survive and lived on the island for nearly 28 years. During that time he discovered what mattered to him in life.

Author

Daniel Defoe worked as a journalist and a novelist. *Robinson Crusoe* was based on the experiences of a real person.

Literary Terms

Foreshadowing: An author's hints about events that will occur later in a story

Adventure: This genre has realistic characters and events but emphasizes action and suspense. The setting is a real place or a place that could be real. The events in the story could happen in real life. Sometimes the action includes a chase or an attempt to find some object or to reach a specific goal.

Other Resources

Book: Defoe, Daniel. *Robinson Crusoe*. Abridged by Robert Blaisdell, et al. (Dover Publications, 1995)

Movies: *Robinson Crusoe* (1996); *Cast Away* (2001)

Web site: www.online-literature.com/defoe/crusoe

The Trojan War

By Carole Gerber

Summary

Paris is determined to marry Helen, the most beautiful woman in the world. But Helen is already married to a powerful king. When Paris and Helen run away together, a war breaks out between the Greeks and the Trojans. Many great warriors on both sides die in battle. Eventually the Greeks think of a trick. They build a giant wooden horse and tell the people of Troy that it is a gift. They use the horse, with soldiers hidden inside, to get inside Troy's walls.

Literary Terms

Epic: A long story about actions, battles, travels, and adventures. The main characters are heroic and larger than life. The story reveals the hero's failings and virtues. The setting covers several nations or the whole world. Gods play an active role in the outcome.

Other Resources

Book: Coolidge, Olivia E. *The Trojan War* (Houghton Mifflin, 2001)

Movie: *Ancient Mysteries: The Odyssey of Troy* (1995)

Web sites: www.encarta.msn.com (Search Trojan War)

www.greekmythology.com/Books/Bulfinch

Monte Cristo's Prison Years

By Linda Lott

Summary

Edmond Dantès was a happy man until he was unjustly imprisoned. Dantès was thrown into the dungeon. One night he heard the scratching sounds of someone trying to escape. This was Abbot Faria, who told Dantès of a treasure in Monte Cristo.

Author

Alexandre Dumas lived an exciting life, so it is no wonder that he wrote such interesting books. Another of his books is *The Three Musketeers*.

Literary Terms

Suspense: Arousing the reader's curiosity or making the reader wonder what will happen next

Irony: The difference between the expected results of a situation and the actual results

Other Resources

Book: Dumas, Alexandre. *The Count of Monte Cristo*. Translated and abridged by Lowell Bair. (Bantam Classic Edition, 1981)

Movie: *The Count of Monte Cristo* (2002)

Web sites: www.literature.org

www.video.go.com/countofmontecristo/intro.htm

Name _____ **Date**_____

The Last Boat
What You Know

Write answers to these questions.

1. If one of your friends or family wanted to do something dangerous, what would you do to try to stop him or her? _____

   _____

2. What makes someone a "loser"?_____

   _____

3. What's hard about learning a new skill or sport? _____

   _____

4. Why do people try to save endangered animals? _____

   _____

There's a Word for It

Choose one of the words in the box to complete each sentence.

capsize	endangered	navigate
current	instinct	spinnaker

1. It can be hard to _____ from one place to another.

2. A large wave can _____ a boat.

3. The sailor's _____ told her the wind was changing.

4. Animals become _____ if their homes are destroyed.

5. The sailboat's _____ caught the wind.

6. The strong _____ pulled the log down the stream.

Word Lists

Chapter	Unfamiliar Words	Word Families	There's a Word for It	Proper Nouns
Chapter 1	attitude instinct pilot promise			Auntie Boom Luis (loo EES) New York City Ruben Sugar Ray
Chapter 2	dangerous erosion expensive loyalty marina pontoon restaurants rickety whether	yacht, yachts	current endangered	Atlantic Ocean Beulah MacDuff Cape Fear River Commodore's Regatta George Zamora (sah MOH rah) Roberto Victorian
Chapter 3	condition hatchlings loggerheads	leather, leatherbacks		Gulf of Mexico Kemp's ridley turtle Oak Island Stumpy
Chapter 4	challenge commercial frothing identify jibing obvious pathetic patience precision technique trophy		capsize instinct navigate, navigation spinnaker	
Chapter 5		criticizes		Independence Day
Chapter 6		buoys		

Name _____ Date_____

The Last Boat
Chapter 1, "Lost Summer"

Fill in the bubble beside the answer for each question.

1. What did Mama make the boys promise?

   Ⓐ They would not get into trouble.

   Ⓑ They would do all their chores.

   Ⓒ They would not go near water.

2. What did Mama try to do in the summer?

   Ⓐ make the boys join a club

   Ⓑ make the boys find a job

   Ⓒ make the boys stay indoors

3. How was Luis like his father?

   Ⓐ He did things his own way.

   Ⓑ He wanted to be a pilot.

   Ⓒ He had the same brown eyes.

4. What did the gang want Luis to do?

   Ⓐ give them money

   Ⓑ stay away

   Ⓒ join them

5. Where did Mama send Luis?

   Ⓐ to his aunt's house

   Ⓑ to summer camp

   Ⓒ to his room

Name _____ Date_____

The Last Boat
Chapter 2, "The River of Fear"

Mark each statement T for True or F for False.

_____ 1. Auntie Boom is not very talkative.

_____ 2. Auntie Boom asks Luis to look at things closely.

_____ 3. Luis misses his life in the city.

_____ 4. Auntie Boom has always saved things, and she promised
to save Luis.

_____ 5. Luis answers all of Auntie Boom's questions.

_____ 6. Luis has never been to the beach before.

_____ 7. Auntie Boom doesn't know very much about nature.

_____ 8. "Boom" is named for her laughter that shakes
windows like thunder.

_____ 9. Luis is looking forward to learning to sail.

_____ 10. To spite Auntie Boom, Luis didn't eat breakfast.

Name _____ Date_____

The Last Boat
Chapter 3, "Escape!"

Fill in the bubble beside the answer for each question.

1. Why does Luis want Auntie Boom to go to sleep?

    Ⓐ so he can go to sleep

    Ⓑ so he can escape

    Ⓒ so he can find his sneakers

2. What happened to the turtle nest?

    Ⓐ Roberto fell on it.

    Ⓑ Luis rode his bike over it.

    Ⓒ Foxes attacked it.

3. Who is Stumpy?

    Ⓐ a leatherback turtle

    Ⓑ a Kemp's ridley turtle

    Ⓒ a loggerhead turtle

4. Why do the boys move away to fight?

    Ⓐ to keep from hurting the eggs

    Ⓑ to get down from the dune

    Ⓒ to get away from the water

5. What is Roberto's secret?

    Ⓐ He stole Luis's sneakers.

    Ⓑ He takes care of the turtle eggs.

    Ⓒ He hates sailing.

Name _____ Date _____

The Last Boat
Chapter 4, "Sailing"

Number the events in order from 1 to 5.

_____ George gives Luis Warning #1.

_____ George teaches Luis and four others the parts of a sailboat.

_____ Luis loses control of the boat and stalls it on a sandbar.

_____ Luis unties his boat and glides away.

_____ George tows the boats around the harbor to show the sailors

the rocks.

Mark each statement T for True or F for False.

_____ 1. Luis learns that *knots* are a way to measure speed and are also

in ropes.

_____ 2. Luis pays close attention to George as he discusses his equipment.

_____ 3. A regatta is a big triangular sail that makes the boat go fast.

_____ 4. Luis challenges the ferryboat with his sailboat.

_____ 5. George says Luis fights the wind and the river.

Name _____ Date_____

The Last Boat
Chapter 5, "Righting the Boat"

Mark each statement T for True or F for False.

_____ 1. Auntie Boom tries to show Luis how to use the wind and the water.

_____ 2. Roberto teaches Luis how to right the boat.

_____ 3. Luis is happy to see Roberto.

_____ 4. Roberto makes Luis capsize the boat on purpose.

_____ 5. Luis follows Roberto's steps exactly.

_____ 6. Luis's way of righting the boat works just as well.

_____ 7. Luis wants to race in the regatta.

_____ 8. Roberto gives back Luis's sneakers.

_____ 9. The sneakers are as good as new.

_____ 10. George tells Luis not to join the race.

Name _____ Date_____

The Last Boat
Chapter 6, "The Last Boat In!"

Number the events in order from 1 to 5.

_____ A boat headed towards Luis.

_____ Luis righted the boat and saved himself.

_____ Wind and rain whipped up and the boat capsized.

_____ Luis decided to enter the race. It was raining slightly.

_____ Luis remembered Roberto's steps.

Mark each statement T for True or F for False.

_____ 1. Luis is ashamed of his sailing skills.

_____ 2. Luis and Auntie Boom watch Roberto race.

_____ 3. Auntie Boom and Luis stay away from the dunes.

_____ 4. Stumpy lays new eggs.

_____ 5. Luis moves the eggs to a safe place.

Name _____ Date_____

The Last Boat
Think About It

Write about or give an oral presentation for each question.

1. Why was the summertime hard for Luis? _____

    _____

2. Was Mama right to send Luis away? Why or why not?_____

    _____

    _____

3. How would things have turned out if Luis had stayed in the city? _____

    _____

Write About It

Choose one of the questions below. Write your answer on a sheet of paper.

1. What was Luis's attitude at the beginning of the summer? How does it change? What difference will his new attitude make when he goes home?

2. Auntie Boom and Roberto loved nature. Luis learned to pay attention to things in nature. Why is it important to protect and respect nature?

3. Do you have a favorite relative? Write about a special time you spent together.

4. A simile is a comparison using *like* or *as*. Find eight similes in the story, and explain them.

The Last Boat

Chapter 1

*Now, I was trouble, a volcano ready to erupt. Trouble found me	12
everywhere. I was smarter than most folks. I tried to do what I was	26
supposed to, but I never could.	32

"Luis, I'm not playing!" Mama would holler. She'd wave her long,	43
skinny finger. "You don't think. You stop fighting or else." But I wasn't	56
gonna sit back and just take it like Ruben did. What good did thinking	70
do him?	72

I had the "fighting instinct" like my father. He died in the war when I	87
was two. At least that's what we always said. Not a street war like with	102
Ruben. There was no real war when our father was in army pilot	115
training. He decided to fly* through a storm.	123

Chapter 6

Stay steady! I know how to talk to the wind. *Don't fight.* I turn the	15
rudder and pull in the sail. Whew!	22

One boat is leading. Another boat is struggling as it heads toward me.	35
I turn, but my sail falls. I switch sides.	44

Wind whips my boat. The rain beats the river. When my boat capsizes,	57
I know it's over. The wind flips the boat on top of me. I try to use my	75
weight to turn it over, but I'm sinking. *Roberto* righted my boat before,	88
not me. It's clear I'm defeated. *Don't I know that I can trust myself?*	102

No one sees me. No one can hear me. The Cape Fear River is	116
thundering. *Just follow the* steps.	121

- The target rate for **Overcoming Adversity** is for students to read 120 words per minute correctly. The asterisks (*) mark 120 words.

- Listen to the student read the passage. Count the number of words read in one minute and the number of errors.

- For the reading rate, subtract the number of errors from the total number of words read.

- Have students enter scores on the Fluency Graph. See page 9.

Building Background

Name _____ Date _____

The Last Boat
What You Know

Write answers to these questions.

1. If one of your friends or family wanted to do something dangerous, what would you do to try to stop him or her? **Ideas: Try to talk my friend out of it or ask my parent or a teacher to help.**

2. What makes someone a "loser"? **Ideas: If the person is afraid to succeed or if the person thinks he or she is inferior to other people**

3. What's hard about learning a new skill or sport? **Ideas: We're afraid to look foolish; we're afraid to fail; it seems too hard to learn.**

4. Why do people try to save endangered animals? **Idea: To keep them from becoming extinct.**

There's a Word for It

Choose one of the words in the box to complete each sentence.

capsize	endangered	navigate
current	instinct	spinnaker

1. It can be hard to ___navigate___ from one place to another.
2. A large wave can ___capsize___ a boat.
3. The sailor's ___instinct___ told her the wind was changing.
4. Animals become ___endangered___ if their homes are destroyed.
5. The sailboat's ___spinnaker___ caught the wind.
6. The strong ___current___ pulled the log down the stream.

Overcoming Adversity • Book 1   15

The Last Boat

Chapter Quiz

Name _____ Date _____

The Last Boat
Chapter 1, "Lost Summer"

Fill in the bubble beside the answer for each question.

1. What did Mama make the boys promise?
   - ● They would not get into trouble.
   - Ⓑ They would do all their chores.
   - Ⓒ They would not go near water.

2. What did Mama try to do in the summer?
   - Ⓐ make the boys join a club
   - Ⓑ make the boys find a job
   - ● make the boys stay indoors

3. How was Luis like his father?
   - ● He did things his own way.
   - Ⓑ He wanted to be a pilot.
   - Ⓒ He had the same brown eyes.

4. What did the gang want Luis to do?
   - Ⓐ give them money
   - Ⓑ stay away
   - ● join them

5. Where did Mama send Luis?
   - ● to his aunt's house
   - Ⓑ to summer camp
   - Ⓒ to his room

Overcoming Adversity • Book 1   17

The Last Boat

Chapter Quiz

Name _____ Date _____

The Last Boat
Chapter 2, "The River of Fear"

Mark each statement T for True or F for False.

___F___ 1. Auntie Boom is not very talkative.

___T___ 2. Auntie Boom asks Luis to look at things closely.

___T___ 3. Luis misses his life in the city.

___T___ 4. Auntie Boom has always saved things, and she promised to save Luis.

___F___ 5. Luis answers all of Auntie Boom's questions.

___F___ 6. Luis has never been to the beach before.

___F___ 7. Auntie Boom doesn't know very much about nature.

___T___ 8. "Boom" is named for her laughter that shakes windows like thunder.

___F___ 9. Luis is looking forward to learning to sail.

___T___ 10. To spite Auntie Boom, Luis didn't eat breakfast.

18   Overcoming Adversity • Book 1

The Last Boat

Chapter Quiz

Name _____ Date _____

The Last Boat
Chapter 3, "Escape!"

Fill in the bubble beside the answer for each question.

1. Why does Luis want Auntie Boom to go to sleep?
   - Ⓐ so he can go to sleep
   - ● so he can escape
   - Ⓒ so he can find his sneakers

2. What happened to the turtle nest?
   - Ⓐ Roberto fell on it.
   - Ⓑ Luis rode his bike over it.
   - ● Foxes attacked it.

3. Who is Stumpy?
   - Ⓐ a leatherback turtle
   - ● a Kemp's ridley turtle
   - Ⓒ a loggerhead turtle

4. Why do the boys move away to fight?
   - ● to keep from hurting the eggs
   - Ⓑ to get down from the dune
   - Ⓒ to get away from the water

5. What is Roberto's secret?
   - Ⓐ He stole Luis's sneakers.
   - ● He takes care of the turtle eggs.
   - Ⓒ He hates sailing.

Overcoming Adversity • Book 1   19

The Last Boat

Answer Key

Name _____ Date _____

The Last Boat
Chapter 4, "Sailing"

Number the events in order from 1 to 5.

__5__ George gives Luis Warning #1.

__1__ George teaches Luis and four others the parts of a sailboat.

__4__ Luis loses control of the boat and stalls it on a sandbar.

__3__ Luis unties his boat and glides away.

__2__ George tows the boats around the harbor to show the sailors the rocks.

Mark each statement T for True or F for False.

__T__ 1. Luis learns that *knots* are a way to measure speed and are also in ropes.

__F__ 2. Luis pays close attention to George as he discusses his equipment.

__F__ 3. A regatta is big triangular sail that makes the boat go fast.

__T__ 4. Luis challenges the ferryboat with his sailboat.

__T__ 5. George says Luis fights the wind and the river.

Overcoming Adversity • Book 1

The Last Boat

Name _____ Date _____

The Last Boat
Chapter 5, "Righting the Boat"

Mark each statement T for True or F for False.

__T__ 1. Auntie Boom tries to show Luis how to use the wind and the water.

__T__ 2. Roberto teaches Luis how to right the boat.

__F__ 3. Luis is happy to see Roberto.

__T__ 4. Roberto makes Luis capsize the boat on purpose.

__F__ 5. Luis follows Roberto's steps exactly.

__F__ 6. Luis's way of righting the boat works just as well.

__F__ 7. Luis wants to race in the regatta.

__T__ 8. Roberto gives back Luis's sneakers.

__F__ 9. The sneakers are as good as new.

__F__ 10. George tells Luis not to join the race.

Overcoming Adversity • Book 1

The Last Boat

Name _____ Date _____

The Last Boat
Chapter 6, "The Last Boat In!"

Number the events in order from 1 to 5.

__2__ A boat headed towards Luis.

__5__ Luis righted the boat and saved himself.

__3__ Wind and rain whipped up and the boat capsized.

__1__ Luis decided to enter the race. It was raining slightly.

__4__ Luis remembered Roberto's steps.

Mark each statement T for True or F for False.

__F__ 1. Luis is ashamed of his sailing skills.

__T__ 2. Luis and Auntie Boom watch Roberto race.

__F__ 3. Auntie Boom and Luis stay away from the dunes.

__T__ 4. Stumpy lays new eggs.

__T__ 5. Luis moves the eggs to a safe place.

Overcoming Adversity • Book 1

The Last Boat

Name _____ Date _____

The Last Boat
Think About It

Write about or give an oral presentation for each question.

1. Why was the summertime hard for Luis? **Ideas: His brother had died in June; it was hot, and Mama wanted him to stay inside; he had no plans.**

2. Was Mama right to send Luis away? Why or why not? **Ideas: Yes, because the summer turned out well for Luis; he did not join the gang. No, because he missed his friends and his life in the city.**

3. How would things have turned out if Luis had stayed in the city? **Ideas: Luis might have joined a gang; Luis might have gotten in trouble.**

Write About It

Choose one of the questions below. Write your answer on a sheet of paper.

1. What was Luis's attitude at the beginning of the summer? How does it change? What difference will his new attitude make when he goes home?

2. Auntie Boom and Roberto loved nature. Luis learned to pay attention to things in nature. Why is it important to protect and respect nature?

3. Do you have a favorite relative? Write about a special time you spent together.

4. A simile is a comparison using *like* or *as*. Find eight similes in the story, and explain them.

Overcoming Adversity • Book 1

The Last Boat

Name _____ Date_____

No Need To Shout
What You Know

Write answers to these questions.

1. When you and a friend have a fight, what do you do to get over it?_____

   _____

2. Have you ever had to start over at a new school? What was hard about

   it? What was good about it?_____

   _____

3. Have people ever warned you about playing with fireworks? What did

   they say? _____

4. A *pun* is the humorous use of one word that sounds like another but

   means something different. Give an example._____

There's a Word for It

Choose one of the words in the box to complete each sentence.

chemicals	experiments	therapy
coma	impaired	unconscious

1. The scientists did _____ to test their ideas.

2. After Jerry broke his leg, he needed physical _____ .

3. Mixing together different _____ is dangerous.

4. She is hearing _____ and uses sign language.

5. Two boys bumped heads, and one was knocked _____.

6. A person in a _____ is unconscious for a long time.

Word Lists

	Unfamiliar Words		Word Families	There's a Word for It	Proper Nouns	
Chapter 1	dangerous dissolve especially finally information oxygen principal process promised science solution though whole		study, student	chemical, chemicals, chemistry experiments	Bunsen burner Jamal Ms. Chin Vernon Williams Middle School	
Chapter 2	cafeteria empty instructions notice oven phone usually					
Chapter 3	favorite funeral guitar radio television vibrated		write, wrote, written	coma		
Chapter 4	apologize communicate counselor deaf gracefully language passengers recognized			impaired therapy unconscious	Amy Greenley School for the Deaf Martin	
Chapter 5	assigned discussions dormitory practice rehabilitation				Evan	
Chapter 6	curious reception worse					

Name _____ Date_____

No Need To Shout
Chapter 1, "A Costly Experiment"

Fill in the bubble beside the answer for each question.

1. What did Jamal think about Vernon?

   Ⓐ He was a loudmouth.

   Ⓑ He liked him.

   Ⓒ both A and B

2. How often was Vernon sent to the office?

   Ⓐ about once a day

   Ⓑ about once a week

   Ⓒ about once a year

3. What did Jamal offer to do?

   Ⓐ help Vernon with his schoolwork

   Ⓑ tell jokes to the class

   Ⓒ help Ms. Chin clean up

4. What did Jamal take to Vernon?

   Ⓐ his backpack

   Ⓑ his hat

   Ⓒ his lunch

5. What did Vernon say Jamal had done?

   Ⓐ made the class laugh

   Ⓑ failed science class

   Ⓒ stolen some chemicals

Name _____ Date_____

No Need to Shout
Chapter 2, "Vernon's Fireworks"

Mark each statement T for True or F for False.

_____ 1. Vernon did not understand why Jamal was so mad.

_____ 2. Jamal was afraid of Vernon.

_____ 3. Vernon planned to make fireworks with the chemicals.

_____ 4. In the past, Vernon had saved Jamal from bullies.

_____ 5. The boys made jokes and puns with the word *peas*.

_____ 6. Jamal went to visit his mom.

_____ 7. Vernon's mother rang the doorbell.

_____ 8. Jamal threw grapes at Vernon.

_____ 9. Vernon forgot about the chemicals he had in the oven.

_____ 10. Jamal turned off the oven just in time.

Name _____ Date_____

No Need to Shout
Chapter 3, "The Sound of Silence"

Fill in the bubble beside the answer for each question.

1. What was wrong with Vernon?

   Ⓐ He could not see.

   Ⓑ He could not hear.

   Ⓒ He had a broken leg.

2. Why did a nurse have to give Vernon a shot?

   Ⓐ to stop his pain

   Ⓑ to calm him down

   Ⓒ to help him eat

3. What had happened to Jamal?

   Ⓐ He moved away.

   Ⓑ He was released from the hospital.

   Ⓒ He was in a coma.

4. Who did Ms. Chin think stole the chemicals?

   Ⓐ Jamal

   Ⓑ Vernon

   Ⓒ one of the bullies

5. How did Vernon feel when his mom said the accident wasn't his fault?

   Ⓐ relieved

   Ⓑ relaxed

   Ⓒ guilty

Name _____ Date _____

No Need to Shout
Chapter 4, "Going to Greenley"

Fill in the bubble beside the answer for each question.

1. What did the doctors say about Vernon?

   Ⓐ   He would never be able to hear.

   Ⓑ   He should learn to sign.

   Ⓒ   both A and B

2. What did Vernon's mother decide?

   Ⓐ   Vernon should go to the boarding school for a year.

   Ⓑ   Vernon could go back to his old school soon.

   Ⓒ   Vernon should not go to school.

3. Who blamed Vernon for Jamal's problems?

   Ⓐ   Vernon

   Ⓑ   Jamal's parents

   Ⓒ   the other students

4. Why did Vernon think he should write a letter?

   Ⓐ   to make sure everyone knew the accident was Jamal's fault

   Ⓑ   to take the blame and clear Jamal's name

   Ⓒ   to make Ms. Chin like him better

5. Why didn't Vernon visit Jamal in the hospital?

   Ⓐ   He couldn't face Jamal.

   Ⓑ   He thought Jamal didn't want to see him.

   Ⓒ   both A and B

Name _____ Date_____

No Need to Shout
Chapter 5, "Good Signs"

Mark each statement T for True or F for False.

_____ 1. Vernon thought classes at Greenley would be easy.

_____ 2. Vernon learned to sign very quickly.

_____ 3. Vernon was afraid to sign in class.

_____ 4. Some students laughed when Vernon made mistakes.

_____ 5. Vernon began to think about how Ms. Chin must have felt.

_____ 6. Vernon wanted to sign something funny to Amy.

_____ 7. All the older boys at Greenley were nice to Vernon.

_____ 8. Some boys signed slowly to make Vernon feel smarter.

_____ 9. Vernon decided to change everything about himself.

_____ 10. Vernon decided it was time to tell the truth about the accident.

Name _____ Date_____

No Need to Shout
Chapter 6, "Peas on Earth"

Mark each statement T for True or F for False

_____ 1. Jamal answered Vernon's letter.

_____ 2. Vernon still did not have many friends at Greenley.

_____ 3. Jamal came to Greenley to tell Vernon what a jerk he was.

_____ 4. Jamal had learned how to sign.

_____ 5. Vernon said he was hurt because Jamal had not visited him in the hospital.

_____ 6. Jamal changed his hairstyle to cornrows.

_____ 7. Ms. Chin gave Jamal a letter to give to Vernon.

_____ 8. Jamal thinks Amy likes Vernon.

_____ 9. Vernon invites Jamal to dinner.

_____ 10. Jamal and Vernon joke about peas again.

Name _____ Date_____

No Need to Shout
Think About It

Write about or give an oral presentation for each question.

1. Have you ever done something that could have harmed you or a friend? What could someone have said or done to stop you? _____

    _____

2. Vernon said, "It's time to grow up." What do you think he meant? _____

    _____

    _____

3. What do you know about learning things from experience? Is it a good way to learn? Why or why not? _____

    _____

Write About It

Choose one of the questions below. Write your answer on a sheet of paper.

1. Pretend you are Vernon and have lost your hearing. Write a letter to your friend Jamal telling him what you miss the most.

2. Find the title *No Need to Shout* in the story, and explain how it is used each time.

3. Much of this story is written in dialogue. Write a conversation between two friends who have had a disagreement.

4. *No Need to Shout* is a coming-of-age story. Describe how the characters changed during the course of the story.

No Need to Shout

Chapter 1

*"I'll see what I can do," Jamal promised as he left the room. He was	15
glad he had helped Ms. Chin, especially after laughing like that at Vernon.	28
As he headed to the principal's office, Jamal thought about the weekend	40
ahead. His mom was picking him up later. He hoped it would be a fun	55
visit. He missed her so much.	61
The past year had been hard. Jamal's father had lost his job. His	74
parents had begun to argue. Then they had split up. Jamal and his dad	88
had moved just a few months ago. His father worked at the new paper	102
mill in town.	105
Also there had been a little trouble with Jamal's grades last year. Well,	118
a *lot** of trouble.	122

Chapter 6

*Jamal said he thought Vernon would visit him when he came out of	13
the coma. But Vernon had left town without a word.	23
Jamal had been angry. He started taking signing lessons during his	34
rehabilitation. He wanted to tell Vernon what a jerk he was when he	47
saw him. But when he got Vernon's letter, he sensed that Vernon was	60
trying to change. Jamal's anger slowly grew less. He wanted to be friends	73
again. He handed Vernon a letter from Ms. Chin to read later.	85
Soon the talk turned to some lighter things. "What happened to your	97
hair?" Jamal asked. "No more dreadlocks."	103
Vernon blushed. "My friend Amy thought that it might look cool this	115
way, with cornrows," he said.*	120

- The target rate for **Overcoming Adversity** is for students to read 120 words per minute correctly. The asterisks (*) mark 120 words.
- Listen to the student read the passage. Count the number of words read in one minute and the number of errors.
- For the reading rate, subtract the number of errors from the total number of words read.
- Have students enter scores on the Fluency Graph. See page 9.

Building Background

Name _____ Date _____

No Need To Shout
What You Know

Write answers to these questions.

1. When you and a friend have a fight, what do you do to get over it? _____
   Ideas: talk it out; listen to each other; apologize

2. Have you ever had to start over at a new school? What was hard about it? What was good about it? **Ideas: Making new friends was hard; having the chance to improve was good.**

3. Have people ever warned you about playing with fireworks? What did they say? **Idea: "You might hurt yourself or someone else."**

4. A *pun* is the humorous use of one word that sounds like another but means something different. Give an example. **Answers will vary.**

There's a Word for It

Choose one of the words in the box to complete each sentence.

chemicals	experiments	therapy
coma	impaired	unconscious

1. The scientists did **experiments** to test their ideas.
2. After Jerry broke his leg, he needed physical **therapy** .
3. Mixing together different **chemicals** is dangerous.
4. She is hearing **impaired** and uses sign language.
5. Two boys bumped heads, and one was knocked **unconscious** .
6. A person in a **coma** is unconscious for a long time.

Overcoming Adversity • Book 2   27

No Need to Shout

Chapter Quiz

Name _____ Date _____

No Need To Shout
Chapter 1, "A Costly Experiment"

Fill in the bubble beside the answer for each question.

1. What did Jamal think about Vernon?
   - Ⓐ He was a loudmouth.
   - Ⓑ He liked him.
   - ● both A and B

2. How often was Vernon sent to the office?
   - Ⓐ about once a day
   - ● about once a week
   - Ⓒ about once a year

3. What did Jamal offer to do?
   - Ⓐ help Vernon with his schoolwork
   - Ⓑ tell jokes to the class
   - ● help Ms. Chin clean up

4. What did Jamal take to Vernon?
   - ● his backpack
   - Ⓑ his hat
   - Ⓒ his lunch

5. What did Vernon say Jamal had done?
   - Ⓐ made the class laugh
   - Ⓑ failed science class
   - ● stolen some chemicals

Overcoming Adversity • Book 2   29

No Need to Shout

Chapter Quiz

Name _____ Date _____

No Need to Shout
Chapter 2, "Vernon's Fireworks"

Mark each statement T for True or F for False.

_T_ 1. Vernon did not understand why Jamal was so mad.

_F_ 2. Jamal was afraid of Vernon.

_T_ 3. Vernon planned to make fireworks with the chemicals.

_T_ 4. In the past, Vernon had saved Jamal from bullies.

_T_ 5. The boys made jokes and puns with the word *peas.*

_F_ 6. Jamal went to visit his mom.

_F_ 7. Vernon's mother rang the doorbell.

_F_ 8. Jamal threw grapes at Vernon.

_T_ 9. Vernon forgot about the chemicals he had in the oven.

_F_ 10. Jamal turned off the oven just in time.

30   Overcoming Adversity • Book 2

No Need to Shout

Chapter Quiz

Name _____ Date _____

No Need to Shout
Chapter 3, "The Sound of Silence"

Fill in the bubble beside the answer for each question.

1. What was wrong with Vernon?
   - Ⓐ He could not see.
   - ● He could not hear.
   - Ⓒ He had a broken leg.

2. Why did a nurse have to give Vernon a shot?
   - Ⓐ to stop his pain
   - ● to calm him down
   - Ⓒ to help him eat

3. What had happened to Jamal?
   - Ⓐ He moved away.
   - Ⓑ He was released from the hospital.
   - ● He was in a coma.

4. Who did Ms. Chin think stole the chemicals?
   - ● Jamal
   - Ⓑ Vernon
   - Ⓒ one of the bullies

5. How did Vernon feel when his mom said the accident wasn't his fault?
   - Ⓐ relieved
   - Ⓑ relaxed
   - ● guilty

Overcoming Adversity • Book 2   31

No Need to Shout

Answer Key

Name _____ Date_____

No Need to Shout
Chapter 4, "Going to Greenley"

Fill in the bubble beside the answer for each question.

1. What did the doctors say about Vernon?
   - (A) He would never be able to hear.
   - (B) He should learn to sign.
   - ● both A and B

2. What did Vernon's mother decide?
   - ● Vernon should go to the boarding school for a year.
   - (B) Vernon could go back to his old school soon.
   - (C) Vernon should not go to school.

3. Who blamed Vernon for Jamal's problems?
   - ● Vernon
   - (B) Jamal's parents
   - (C) the other students

4. Why did Vernon think he should write a letter?
   - (A) to make sure everyone knew the accident was Jamal's fault
   - ● to take the blame and clear Jamal's name
   - (C) to make Ms. Chin like him better

5. Why didn't Vernon visit Jamal in the hospital?
   - (A) He couldn't face Jamal.
   - (B) He thought Jamal didn't want to see him.
   - ● both A and B

32   Overcoming Adversity • Book 2

No Need to Shout

Name _____ Date_____

No Need to Shout
Chapter 5, "Good Signs"

Mark each statement T for True or F for False.

F   1. Vernon thought classes at Greenley would be easy.

F   2. Vernon learned to sign very quickly.

T   3. Vernon was afraid to sign in class.

T   4. Some students laughed when Vernon made mistakes.

T   5. Vernon began to think about how Ms. Chin must have felt.

T   6. Vernon wanted to sign something funny to Amy.

F   7. All the older boys at Greenley were nice to Vernon.

F   8. Some boys signed slowly to make Vernon feel smarter.

F   9. Vernon decided to change everything about himself.

T   10. Vernon decided it was time to tell the truth about the accident.

Overcoming Adversity • Book 2   33

No Need to Shout

Name _____ Date_____

No Need to Shout
Chapter 6, "Peas on Earth"

Mark each statement T for True or F for False

F   1. Jamal answered Vernon's letter.

F   2. Vernon still did not have many friends at Greenley.

F   3. Jamal came to Greenley to tell Vernon what a jerk he was.

T   4. Jamal had learned how to sign.

F   5. Vernon said he was hurt because Jamal had not visited him
      in the hospital.

F   6. Jamal changed his hairstyle to cornrows.

T   7. Ms. Chin gave Jamal a letter to give to Vernon.

T   8. Jamal thinks Amy likes Vernon.

T   9. Vernon invites Jamal to dinner.

T   10. Jamal and Vernon joke about peas again.

34   Overcoming Adversity • Book 2

No Need to Shout

Name _____ Date_____

No Need to Shout
Think About It

Write about or give an oral presentation for each question.

1. Have you ever done something that could have harmed you or a friend? What could someone have said or done to stop you? **Answers will vary.**

   _____

2. Vernon said, "It's time to grow up." What do you think he meant? **Ideas: He meant he would become a better person and a better friend; he would take responsibility for what he had done.**

3. What do you know about learning things from experience? Is it a good way to learn? Why or why not? **Ideas: Sometimes learning from experience is dangerous. You might not get a second chance.**

Write About It

Choose one of the questions below. Write your answer on a sheet of paper.

1. Pretend you are Vernon and have lost your hearing. Write a letter to your friend Jamal telling him what you miss the most.

2. Find the title *No Need to Shout* in the story, and explain how it is used each time.

3. Much of this story is written in dialogue. Write a conversation between two friends who have had a disagreement.

4. *No Need to Shout* is a coming-of-age story. Describe how the characters changed during the course of the story.

Overcoming Adversity • Book 2   35

No Need to Shout

Name _____ Date_____

Playing Through Pain
What You Know

Write answers to these questions.

1. What is your favorite sport? What makes it exciting? _____

   _____

2. What is a role model? How should a role model act?_____

   _____

3. Whom do we expect to be role models? _____

   _____

4. If you became famous and wealthy, how would you spend your money

   and time?_____

   _____

There's a Word for It

Choose one of the words in the box to complete each sentence.

contract	javelin	respect
draft	mourn	survivors

1. The terrible flood left many _____ homeless.

2. A _____ is an agreement that can be legally enforced.

3. The _____ is a light spear.

4. Many people feel sad and _____ when a pet dies.

5. Sports teams try to select, or _____, the best players.

6. Some people win _____ through hard work.

Word Lists

	Unfamiliar Words	Word Families	There's a Word for It	Proper Nouns
Chapter 1	announcer, human, radio	Puerto Rico, Puerto Rican		Latino, New York, Pirates, Pittsburgh, Roberto Clemente (roh BAYR toh clah MAYN tay)
Chapter 2	bought, business, college, finally, honest, importance, muscles, practicing, taught, though, value		javelin, respect	Carolina, Olympics, Spanish
Chapter 3	bonus, promised, talent, uniform		contract, draft	Brooklyn Dodgers, English, French, Montreal, United States
Chapter 4	athlete, autographs, competition, despite, headaches, hero, honor, malaria, stadium, surgery, television, terrible		injury, injuries, injured	Gold Glove, Most Valuable Player, National League, World Series
Chapter 5	artificial, citizens, deaf, donated, expensive, extra, furniture, notice, special			Nicaragua (nee cah RAH gwah), Vera
Chapter 6	acres, earthquake, equipment, period, prepare, relief, soccer, statue, usually		fly, flown, mourn, survivors	Baseball Hall of Fame, Christmas

Overcoming Adversity • Book 3

Name _____ Date_____

Playing Through Pain
Chapter 1, "Born to Play"

Mark each statement T for True or F for False.

_____ **1.** Roberto said he was born to fly planes.

_____ **2.** As a boy, Roberto sometimes used a tin can as a baseball.

_____ **3.** By the time he was 19, Roberto was in the big leagues.

_____ **4.** Roberto played for the Pittsburgh Pirates.

_____ **5.** Roberto hit mostly to right field.

_____ **6.** Roberto was known for his fast pitch.

_____ **7.** Roberto is considered one of the greatest baseball players ever.

_____ **8.** Roberto wasn't a very nice person.

_____ **9.** Roberto was ashamed of his Puerto Rican roots.

_____ **10.** Roberto's parents taught him right from wrong.

Name _____ **Date** _____

Playing Through Pain
Chapter 2, "Baseball Kid"

Fill in the bubble beside the answer for each question.

1. What language did Roberto's family speak?

    Ⓐ French

    Ⓑ English

    Ⓒ Spanish

2. Where did Roberto's father work?

    Ⓐ in a baseball team office

    Ⓑ in the sugarcane fields

    Ⓒ in a grocery store

3. How did Roberto earn money to pay for a bike?

    Ⓐ delivering newspapers

    Ⓑ delivering milk

    Ⓒ picking up pennies

4. What did Roberto learn from his job?

    Ⓐ Hard work feels good.

    Ⓑ Work is no fun.

    Ⓒ It is easy to make money.

5. What did Roberto's parents want their son to do?

    Ⓐ go to college

    Ⓑ be an engineer

    Ⓒ both A and B

Name _____ Date_____

Playing Through Pain
Chapter 3, "A Dream Come True"

Number the events in order from 1 to 5.

_____ Roberto wanted to quit because he never got to play.

_____ Roberto made $40 a week playing baseball in the winter leagues.

_____ Roberto began playing on a baseball team.

_____ A softball coach saw Roberto hit tin cans.

_____ At age 14, Roberto made the softball team.

Number the events in order from 6 to 10.

_____ Roberto signed a contract to play for the Dodgers.

_____ Major league scouts came to Puerto Rico looking for new players.

_____ The Pittsburgh Pirates drafted Roberto.

_____ The Dodgers tried to hide Roberto.

_____ Roberto played in the minor leagues in Montreal.

Name _____ **Date** _____

Playing Through Pain
Chapter 4, "Baseball Hero"

Fill in the bubble beside the answer for each question.

1. How long did Roberto play for the Pirates?

   Ⓐ 1 year

   Ⓑ 8 years

   Ⓒ 18 years

2. What did reporters say about Roberto?

   Ⓐ He was a "hot dog."

   Ⓑ He spoke English badly.

   Ⓒ both A and B

3. How did Roberto treat the fans?

   Ⓐ He played catch with them.

   Ⓑ He was rude to them.

   Ⓒ He spent time talking with them.

4. What did Roberto do when he was not named Most Valuable Player?

   Ⓐ threw his bat

   Ⓑ worked harder

   Ⓒ blamed the coach

5. Why do people remember Roberto's last hit in 1972?

   Ⓐ It was a grand slam.

   Ⓑ It was his 3,000th hit.

   Ⓒ It won the World Series.

Name _____ Date_____

Playing Through Pain
Chapter 5, "Off-Field Hero"

Mark each statement T for True or F for False.

_____ 1. Every winter Roberto went to Hawaii.

_____ 2. Roberto met his wife in Puerto Rico.

_____ 3. Vera and Roberto had three girls.

_____ 4. Roberto taught children to play baseball.

_____ 5. Roberto told children to be good citizens.

_____ 6. Roberto did not like being a role model for children.

_____ 7. Not many people came to Roberto Clemente Night at Three Rivers Stadium.

_____ 8. Roberto was proud to be Latino.

_____ 9. A salesman thought Roberto was poor because he was Latino.

_____ 10. Roberto liked to talk about the good things he did.

Name _____ **Date** _____

Playing Through Pain
Chapter 6, "Last Season"

Number the events in order from 1 to 5.

_____ An earthquake hit Nicaragua.

_____ Roberto heard that supplies were not getting to the people who
needed them.

_____ Roberto wanted to work on plans for a new sports center.

_____ Roberto collected food and clothes to help earthquake victims.

_____ After the baseball season, Roberto went home to Puerto Rico.

Number the events in order from 6 to 10.

_____ To honor Roberto's dream, people gave money to build Sports City.

_____ Roberto decided to take the supplies to Nicaragua himself.

_____ On New Year's Eve, the plane crashed.

_____ Roberto became the first Latino voted into baseball's Hall of Fame.

_____ The relief plane was too heavy when it took off.

Name _____ Date_____

Playing Through Pain
Think About It

Write about or give an oral presentation for each question.

1. If Roberto had not died on the plane, what do you think he would be doing today? _____

2. Give examples from the book to explain the title *Playing Through Pain.*

   _____

   _____

3. What are some lessons Roberto learned from his parents?_____

   _____

4. Roberto's nickname was "The Great One." What would yours be? Why?

   _____

Write About It

Choose one of the questions below. Write your answer on a sheet of paper.

1. Make a trading card about yourself. Draw your picture. Write about things you have done.

2. You are a role model for younger children. What advice would you give to them?

3. It is Roberto Clemente Day at your school. You will give a speech about Roberto's life. Tell why people remember him.

4. If you have read *Once There Were Two,* compare it to *Playing Through Pain.*

Playing Through Pain

Chapter 2

*Roberto's father, like most others, worked in the sugarcane fields.	10
He was in charge of a crew of men who cut cane. Even though it was	26
hard, hot work, he did not make enough money to support his family.	39
He had to find a second job. He used an old truck to haul sand, gravel,	55
and other goods.	58
Roberto's mom worked too. She ran a grocery store. People who	69
worked in the fields bought things they needed from her store. Still, the	82
family did not have much money.	88
Roberto loved his parents. They taught him to be good and kind. They	101
taught him the importance of being honest. His parents taught him to	113
respect adults and to help others. They* showed him the value of hard	126
work.	127

Chapter 5

*Even though it wasn't easy to be Latino in his time, Roberto was	13
proud of his roots. When the players stopped to eat, some places would	26
serve only whites. Only whites could stay in many of the hotels. Roberto	39
and others spoke up. This was unfair! They did not want to be treated	53
in this way. But these problems did not prevent Roberto from playing	65
well.	66
Even when he was not playing baseball, Roberto and his family were	78
treated unfairly. Once he and his wife went furniture shopping. The	89
expensive furniture was on the first floor of the store. Cheaper furniture	101
was on the upper floors.	106
Roberto wanted to buy some furniture on the first floor. The salesman	118
said, "I* think we have something better for you on the sixth floor."	131

- The target rate for **Overcoming Adversity** is for students to read 120 words per minute correctly. The asterisks (*) mark 120 words.

- Listen to the student read the passage. Count the number of words read in one minute and the number of errors.

- For the reading rate, subtract the number of errors from the total number of words read.

- Have students enter scores on the Fluency Graph. See page 9.

Building Background

Name _____ Date _____

Playing Through Pain
What You Know

Write answers to these questions.

1. What is your favorite sport? What makes it exciting? **Answers will vary.**

    _____

2. What is a role model? How should a role model act? **Ideas: A role model is someone we look up to; a role model sets a good example.**

3. Whom do we expect to be role models? **Ideas: parents, teachers, sports heroes, entertainers, and public officials**

4. If you became famous and wealthy, how would you spend your money and time? **Ideas: Buy things for myself; would donate time and money to charity**

There's a Word for It

Choose one of the words in the box to complete each sentence.

contract	javelin	respect
draft	mourn	survivors

1. The terrible flood left many **survivors** homeless.
2. A **contract** is an agreement that can be legally enforced.
3. The **javelin** is a light spear.
4. Many people feel sad and **mourn** when a pet dies.
5. Sports teams try to select, or **draft**, the best players.
6. Some people win **respect** through hard work.

Overcoming Adversity • Book 3   39

Playing Through Pain

Chapter Quiz

Name _____ Date _____

Playing Through Pain
Chapter 1, "Born to Play"

Mark each statement T for True or F for False.

F 1. Roberto said he was born to fly planes.

T 2. As a boy, Roberto sometimes used a tin can as a baseball.

T 3. By the time he was 19, Roberto was in the big leagues.

T 4. Roberto played for the Pittsburgh Pirates.

F 5. Roberto hit mostly to right field.

F 6. Roberto was known for his fast pitch.

T 7. Roberto is considered one of the greatest baseball players ever.

F 8. Roberto wasn't a very nice person.

F 9. Roberto was ashamed of his Puerto Rican roots.

T 10. Roberto's parents taught him right from wrong.

Overcoming Adversity • Book 3   41

Playing Through Pain

Chapter Quiz

Name _____ Date _____

Playing Through Pain
Chapter 2, "Baseball Kid"

Fill in the bubble beside the answer for each question.

1. What language did Roberto's family speak?
    - Ⓐ French
    - Ⓑ English
    - ● Spanish

2. Where did Roberto's father work?
    - Ⓐ in a baseball team office
    - ● in the sugarcane fields
    - Ⓒ in a grocery store

3. How did Roberto earn money to pay for a bike?
    - Ⓐ delivering newspapers
    - ● delivering milk
    - Ⓒ picking up pennies

4. What did Roberto learn from his job?
    - ● Hard work feels good.
    - Ⓑ Work is no fun.
    - Ⓒ It is easy to make money.

5. What did Roberto's parents want their son to do?
    - Ⓐ go to college
    - Ⓑ be an engineer
    - ● both A and B

42   Overcoming Adversity • Book 3

Playing Through Pain

Chapter Quiz

Name _____ Date _____

Playing Through Pain
Chapter 3, "A Dream Come True"

Number the events in order from 1 to 5.

5 Roberto wanted to quit because he never got to play.

4 Roberto made $40 a week playing baseball in the winter leagues.

3 Roberto began playing on a baseball team.

1 A softball coach saw Roberto hit tin cans.

2 At age 14, Roberto made the softball team.

Number the events in order from 6 to 10.

7 Roberto signed a contract to play for the Dodgers.

6 Major league scouts came to Puerto Rico looking for new players.

10 The Pittsburgh Pirates drafted Roberto.

9 The Dodgers tried to hide Roberto.

8 Roberto played in the minor leagues in Montreal.

Overcoming Adversity • Book 3   43

Playing Through Pain

Overcoming Adversity • Book 3   **49**

Answer Key

Name _____ Date_____

Once There Were Two
What You Know

Write answers to these questions.

1. Who are your favorite sports stars? Why do you think they are famous?

   _____

2. What do you know about segregation? _____

   _____

3. What is prejudice? _____

   _____

4. Why do you think some people are prejudiced? _____

   _____

There's a Word for It

Choose one of the words in the box to complete each sentence.

integrate	morally	segregation
league	prejudiced	tall tale

1. To be _____ is to have an opinion not based on facts.

2. The story of Paul Bunyan is really a _____.

3. Dad's softball team competed in a local _____.

4. To _____ is to bring different races together.

5. _____ kept African Americans apart from whites.

6. He always did the right thing; he behaved _____.

Word Lists

	Unfamiliar Words	Word Families	There's a Word for It	Proper Nouns
Chapter 1	famous, favorite, heroes, separate, special	League—American, Eastern Colored, National, Negro; muscle, muscular; respect, respected	league, segregation, segregated	Babe Ruth, Griffith Stadium, James "Cool Papa" Bell, Jimmie Crutchfield, Josh Gibson, Leroy "Satchel" Paige, New York Yankees, Oscar Charleston, Pittsburgh Crawfords, Washington, D.C., William Julius "Judy" Johnson
Chapter 2	accidentally, continued, guards, influence, injured	Stockings—Chicago White, Toledo Blue; recruit, recruited	prejudiced	Adrian Constantine, Brooklyn, Cherokee, Chief Tokahoma, Confederate, George Stovey, Jackie Robinson, Knickerbockers, Moses Fleetwood "Fleet" Walker, National Association of Baseball Players, New Jersey, Philadelphia, Union
Chapter 3	businesses, challenges, character, developed, professional, restaurants, stomachs, theaters, though			Great Depression, Michigan, U.S. Supreme Court
Chapter 4	determined, expressive, hesitation, interviews, positions, schedules		tall tale	Arkansas, Cuban Stars, Detroit Stars, J. L. Wilkinson, Kansas City Monarchs, Martin Dihigo, Mexico, Rube Foster, St. Louis Giants
Chapter 5	climate, competitions, ghost, guests, philosophy, regular, usually			Babe Didrickson, Branch Rickey, Dizzy Dean, Jesse Owens, Newark Eagles, Puerto Rico, Spanish, Venezuela
Chapter 6	barrier, haunted, humiliation, promised, situation		integrate, morally	Brooklyn Dodgers, Charlie Thomas, Don Newcombe, Roy Campanella

Name _____ Date_____

Once There Were Two
Chapter 1, "Unknown Sports Heroes"

Mark each statement T for True or F for False.

_____ 1. Many people in 1936 did not have time for baseball.

_____ 2. Babe Ruth hit 46 home runs to set the American League record.

_____ 3. Babe Ruth's home run record beat Josh Gibson's record.

_____ 4. Babe Ruth was called "the white Josh Gibson."

_____ 5. Josh Gibson played in the Negro Leagues.

_____ 6. Many experts say the best baseball team ever was the Pittsburgh Crawfords.

_____ 7. Leroy "Satchel" Paige is considered one of the greatest pitchers of all time.

_____ 8. Starting in 1920, black ballplayers played in the major leagues.

_____ 9. African American players did not want to play in the major leagues.

_____ 10. White fans did not go to Negro League games.

Name _____ Date_____

Once There Were Two
Chapter 2, "Play Ball!"

Fill in the bubble beside the answer for each question.

1. Where do most people believe the first baseball game was played?

   Ⓐ California

   Ⓑ New Jersey

   Ⓒ Ohio

2. What helped spread the game of baseball throughout the country?

   Ⓐ newspapers

   Ⓑ radio

   Ⓒ the Civil War

3. Why did John W. "Bud" Fowler invent the first shin guards?

   Ⓐ Fowler hurt his legs sliding into base.

   Ⓑ White players "accidentally" stuck their spikes into his legs.

   Ⓒ Fowler wanted to keep balls from bouncing into his shins.

4. Which coach refused to allow his white players to play against teams
   with African American players?

   Ⓐ "Fleet" Walker

   Ⓑ Babe Ruth

   Ⓒ Cap Anson

5. Who was the first black player in the major leagues?

   Ⓐ Moses Fleetwood "Fleet" Walker

   Ⓑ Leroy "Satchel" Paige

   Ⓒ Josh Gibson

Name _____ **Date**_____

Once There Were Two
Chapter 3, "How Baseball Built Communities"

Fill in the bubble beside the answer for each question.

1. What did "Jim Crow" laws do?

   Ⓐ gave everyone the same rights

   Ⓑ took away black people's rights

   Ⓒ let cities start baseball teams

2. What did the Supreme Court rule in 1896?

   Ⓐ It was legal to keep black people "separate but equal."

   Ⓑ Anyone could play baseball.

   Ⓒ both A and B

3. Where did the first black professional team start?

   Ⓐ Atlanta, Georgia

   Ⓑ New York City

   Ⓒ Los Angeles, California

4. Why did the Giants sleep on the train?

   Ⓐ They could not stay in most hotels because they were African American.

   Ⓑ They could get to the games faster.

   Ⓒ They were tired from playing baseball and needed to sleep right away.

5. What did the black teams do for black people?

   Ⓐ gave black people jobs

   Ⓑ gave black children role models

   Ⓒ both A and B

Name _____ Date _____

Once There Were Two
Chapter 4, "A Roster of Greats"

Mark each statement T for True or F for False.

_____ 1. James "Cool Papa" Bell was the fastest man in baseball.

_____ 2. Cool Papa could beat his own ball to second base.

_____ 3. Josh Gibson had the highest lifetime batting average in the Negro Leagues.

_____ 4. Martin Dihigo could play all nine positions and won three home run crowns.

_____ 5. Dihigo is in the Baseball Hall of Fame in three countries.

_____ 6. Satchel Paige was too busy being funny to be a good pitcher.

_____ 7. The "father of black baseball" is Rube Foster of the Chicago Giants.

_____ 8. Foster and seven others formed the Negro National League.

_____ 9. Foster was able to keep whites from owning black baseball teams.

_____ 10. Each state had just one Negro League team.

Name _____ Date_____

Once There Were Two
Chapter 5, "Equals on the Field"

Fill in the bubble beside the answer for each question.

1. Black and white teams played each other in "barnstorming" games, which were

   Ⓐ games played in another country.

   Ⓑ traveling games played all over the United States.

   Ⓒ games played without the usual rules.

2. Why did white all-star teams play against black teams?

   Ⓐ to help end segregation

   Ⓑ to make black players look bad

   Ⓒ to make money in the off-season

3. Which teams won most of those games?

   Ⓐ White teams won eighty percent of the time.

   Ⓑ Black teams won sixty percent of the time.

   Ⓒ They each won an equal number.

4. What did the Negro Leagues do to bring in fans?

   Ⓐ They rigged lights and played at night.

   Ⓑ They played blindfolded, invented "ghost ball," and had special guests.

   Ⓒ both A and B

5. Who played on Mexican baseball teams?

   Ⓐ players of all races

   Ⓑ only black players

   Ⓒ only white players and Mexicans

Name _____ **Date**_____

Once There Were Two
Chapter 6, "A Beginning and an End"

Mark each statement T for True or F for False.

_____ 1. Branch Rickey felt segregation was right.

_____ 2. Some people threatened Jackie Robinson's life.

_____ 3. Satchel Paige never got the chance to play in the major leagues.

_____ 4. After blacks started to play on major league teams, the Negro
Leagues still drew large crowds.

_____ 5. The Negro Leagues played an important part in baseball history.

Number the events in order from 1 to 5.

_____ The Negro Leagues ended.

_____ Robinson was named the league's Rookie of the Year and later
Most Valuable Player.

_____ Branch Rickey became manager of the Brooklyn Dodgers in 1942.

_____ Other major league teams signed black players.

_____ Rickey signed Jackie Robinson to play for the Dodgers.

Name _____ Date_____

Once There Were Two
Think About It

Write about or give an oral presentation for each question.

1. At one time there was a "color barrier" in major league baseball. What other "barriers" have we had to overcome? _____

    _____

2. What other areas of society had "barriers"? Are all the "barriers" gone?

    _____

    _____

3. How did segregation hurt the major leagues? _____

    _____

4. Why did Branch Rickey fight to get an African American player on his team? _____

    _____

Write About It

Choose one of the questions below. Write your answer on a sheet of paper.

1. Make up a sports "hall of fame" with players of all genders and races.

2. Find out more about one of the players named in the book. Write a report on that player.

3. Learn more about Jackie Robinson. Then write about how it might have felt to be the first black major league player.

4. Relate the story of the Negro Leagues to the theme **Overcoming Adversity.**

Once There Were Two

Chapter 1

*His right sleeve was rolled above his muscular forearm. The brim of	12
his cap was pushed back. His large body looked relaxed.	22
But the fans weren't fooled. They could read the look on his face. It	36
sent them a clear message: "I'm going to do it again."	47
"It" was hitting a home run. The fans wished for it as much as the man	63
did. Whack! They got their wish sooner than they expected.	73
The batter hit the first pitch high toward center field. It cleared the	86
fence and sailed right out of the park. The fans went wild. They yelled.	100
They jumped. They hugged. Some threw their hats in the air.	111
Any home run would be cause for joy. But* this one was special.	124

Chapter 6

*Satchel Paige was the exception. He was around 40 in 1948 when	12
Cleveland signed him. He pitched his last major league game in 1965.	24
He was around 57 years old!	30
Major league teams had the cash to bring the best black players to the	44
majors. Black fans wanted to watch the top players. The Negro Leagues	56
could not afford the top players, so fewer and fewer fans came to the	70
games. When they started, the Negro Leagues gave black players a	81
place to play baseball. After black players were accepted in the major	93
leagues, the Negro Leagues folded.	98
The Negro Leagues were an important part of baseball history. They	109
showed that black players were as good as white players and* that	111
they deserved to play in the same league.	129

- The target rate for **Overcoming Adversity** is for students to read 120 words per minute correctly. The asterisks (*) mark 120 words.

- Listen to the student read the passage. Count the number of words read in one minute and the number of errors.

- For the reading rate, subtract the number of errors from the total number of words read.

- Have students enter scores on the Fluency Graph. See page 9.

Name _____ Date_____

Once There Were Two
What You Know

Write answers to these questions.

1. Who are your favorite sports stars? Why do you think they are famous?
   Answers will vary.

2. What do you know about segregation? _____
   Answers will vary.

3. What is prejudice? **Idea: Prejudice is making up your mind without considering the facts.**

4. Why do you think some people are prejudiced? **Idea: Prejudiced people are afraid or are taught to believe certain things.**

There's a Word for It

Choose one of the words in the box to complete each sentence.

integrate	morally	segregation
league	prejudiced	tall tale

1. To be ___**prejudiced**___ is to have an opinion not based on facts.
2. The story of Paul Bunyan is really a ___**tall tale**___.
3. Dad's softball team competed in a local ___**league**___.
4. To ___**integrate**___ is to bring different races together.
5. ___**Segregation**___ kept African Americans apart from whites.
6. He always did the right thing; he behaved ___**morally**___

Name _____ Date_____

Once There Were Two
Chapter 1, "Unknown Sports Heroes"

Mark each statement T for True or F for False.

__F__ 1. Many people in 1936 did not have time for baseball.

__T__ 2. Babe Ruth hit 46 home runs to set the American League record.

__F__ 3. Babe Ruth's home run record beat Josh Gibson's record.

__F__ 4. Babe Ruth was called "the white Josh Gibson."

__T__ 5. Josh Gibson played in the Negro Leagues.

__T__ 6. Many experts say the best baseball team ever was the Pittsburgh Crawfords.

__T__ 7. Leroy "Satchel" Paige is considered one of the greatest pitchers of all time.

__F__ 8. Starting in 1920, black ballplayers played in the major leagues.

__F__ 9. African American players did not want to play in the major leagues.

__F__ 10. White fans did not go to Negro League games.

Name _____ Date_____

Once There Were Two
Chapter 2, "Play Ball!"

Fill in the bubble beside the answer for each question.

1. Where do most people believe the first baseball game was played?
   - Ⓐ California
   - ● New Jersey
   - Ⓒ Ohio

2. What helped spread the game of baseball throughout the country?
   - Ⓐ newspapers
   - Ⓑ radio
   - ● the Civil War

3. Why did John W. "Bud" Fowler invent the first shin guards?
   - Ⓐ Fowler hurt his legs sliding into base.
   - ● White players "accidentally" stuck their spikes into his legs.
   - Ⓒ Fowler wanted to keep balls from bouncing into his shins.

4. Which coach refused to allow his white players to play against teams with African American players?
   - Ⓐ "Fleet" Walker
   - Ⓑ Babe Ruth
   - ● Cap Anson

5. Who was the first black player in the major leagues?
   - ● Moses Fleetwood "Fleet" Walker
   - Ⓑ Leroy "Satchel" Paige
   - Ⓒ Josh Gibson

Name _____ Date_____

Once There Were Two
Chapter 3, "How Baseball Built Communities"

Fill in the bubble beside the answer for each question.

1. What did "Jim Crow" laws do?
   - Ⓐ gave everyone the same rights
   - ● took away black people's rights
   - Ⓒ let cities start baseball teams

2. What did the Supreme Court rule in 1896?
   - ● It was legal to keep black people "separate but equal."
   - Ⓑ Anyone could play baseball.
   - Ⓒ both A and B

3. Where did the first black professional team start?
   - Ⓐ Atlanta, Georgia
   - ● New York City
   - Ⓒ Los Angeles, California

4. Why did the Giants sleep on the train?
   - ● They could not stay in most hotels because they were African American.
   - Ⓑ They could get to the games faster.
   - Ⓒ They were tired from playing baseball and needed to sleep right away.

5. What did the black teams do for black people?
   - Ⓐ gave black people jobs
   - Ⓑ gave black children role models
   - ● both A and B

Answer Key

Once There Were Two

Name _____ Date _____

Once There Were Two
Chapter 4, "A Roster of Greats"

Mark each statement T for True or F for False.

__T__ 1. James "Cool Papa" Bell was the fastest man in baseball.

__F__ 2. Cool Papa could beat his own ball to second base.

__T__ 3. Josh Gibson had the highest lifetime batting average in the
Negro Leagues.

__T__ 4. Martin Dihigo could play all nine positions and won three
home run crowns.

__T__ 5. Dihigo is in the Baseball Hall of Fame in three countries.

__F__ 6. Satchel Paige was too busy being funny to be a good pitcher.

__T__ 7. The "father of black baseball" is Rube Foster of the
Chicago Giants.

__T__ 8. Foster and seven others formed the Negro National League.

__F__ 9. Foster was able to keep whites from owning black baseball teams.

__F__ 10. Each state had just one Negro League team.

Overcoming Adversity • Book 4

Name _____ Date _____

Once There Were Two
Chapter 5, "Equals on the Field"

Fill in the bubble beside the answer for each question.

1. Black and white teams played each other in "barnstorming" games,
which were
   - Ⓐ games played in another country.
   - ● traveling games played all over the United States.
   - Ⓒ games played without the usual rules.

2. Why did white all-star teams play against black teams?
   - Ⓐ to help end segregation
   - Ⓑ to make black players look bad
   - ● to make money in the off-season

3. Which teams won most of those games?
   - Ⓐ White teams won eighty percent of the time.
   - ● Black teams won sixty percent of the time.
   - Ⓒ They each won an equal number.

4. What did the Negro Leagues do to bring in fans?
   - Ⓐ They rigged lights and played at night.
   - Ⓑ They played blindfolded, invented "ghost ball," and had
special guests.
   - ● both A and B

5. Who played on Mexican baseball teams?
   - ● players of all races
   - Ⓑ only black players
   - Ⓒ only white players and Mexicans

Overcoming Adversity • Book 4

Name _____ Date _____

Once There Were Two
Chapter 6, "A Beginning and an End"

Mark each statement T for True or F for False.

__F__ 1. Branch Rickey felt segregation was right.

__T__ 2. Some people threatened Jackie Robinson's life.

__F__ 3. Satchel Paige never got the chance to play in the major leagues.

__F__ 4. After blacks started to play on major league teams, the Negro
Leagues still drew large crowds.

__T__ 5. The Negro Leagues played an important part in baseball history.

Number the events in order from 1 to 5.

__5__ The Negro Leagues ended.

__3__ Robinson was named the league's Rookie of the Year and later
Most Valuable Player.

__1__ Branch Rickey became manager of the Brooklyn Dodgers in 1942.

__4__ Other major league teams signed black players.

__2__ Rickey signed Jackie Robinson to play for the Dodgers.

Overcoming Adversity • Book 4

Name _____ Date _____

Once There Were Two
Think About It

Write about or give an oral presentation for each question.

1. At one time there was a "color barrier" in major league baseball. What
other "barriers" have we had to overcome? __Ideas: gender, religious,__
__economic, age, and ethnic background__

2. What other areas of society had "barriers"? Are all the "barriers" gone?
__Ideas: business, sports, education, military, astronaut training.__
__Probably not, because people still have prejudices.__

3. How did segregation hurt the major leagues? __Idea: They missed out on many__
__good players and on loyal fans and money.__

4. Why did Branch Rickey fight to get an African American player on his
team? __Ideas: He saw how segregation hurt people; he knew black__
__players would be good for baseball.__

Write About It

Choose one of the questions below. Write your answer on a sheet of paper.

1. Make up a sports "hall of fame" with players of all genders and races.

2. Find out more about one of the players named in the book. Write a
report on that player.

3. Learn more about Jackie Robinson. Then write about how it might have
felt to be the first black major league player.

4. Relate the story of the Negro Leagues to the theme **Overcoming
Adversity.**

Overcoming Adversity • Book 4

Name _____ Date_____

Walls of Water
What You Know

Write answers to these questions.

1. Name some natural disasters. _____

   _____

2. What should you do when you hear a disaster warning? _____

   _____

3. What do some people do when they hear this kind of warning? _____

   _____

4. Choose a natural disaster, and explain how it can be prevented or

   controlled._____

   _____

There's a Word for It

Choose one of the words in the box to complete each sentence.

debris	levee	tsunami
disaster	tragedy	victims

1. A _____ is a tidal wave.

2. The _____ that the flood left behind littered the streets.

3. A serious misfortune or terrible event is a _____.

4. The flood _____ lost their homes.

5. We built a strong _____ to hold back high water.

6. A tornado is a natural _____ that can destroy homes.

Word Lists

	Unfamiliar Words	Word Families	There's a Word for It	Proper Nouns	
	able boulders collapsed destroyed ruins	flood, floods, flooding survivor, survivors	debris (de BREE)	Johnstown Pennsylvania Stony Creek River	**Chapter 1**
	clothing relatives rescue thousands	build, building, built, rebuilt	disaster tragedy victims	American Red Cross Children's Aid Society Clara Barton	**Chapter 2**
	attracted businesses channel property route	area, areas worse, worst		Cambria Iron Company Conemaugh River (KAH neh maw)	**Chapter 3**
	operate system	effect, effects	levee (LEH vee)	Gulf of Mexico Minnesota Mississippi River Basin National Weather Service	**Chapter 4**
	acres effort recovered			National Guard Ohio Valley	**Chapter 5**
	example predicting	type, types	tsunami (soo NAH mee)	Belgium England Hawaii Netherlands	**Chapter 6**

Name _____ Date _____

Walls of Water
Chapter 1, "The Johnstown Flood, 1889"

Number the events in order from 1 to 5.

_____ Tons of lumber rolled down the river.

_____ It rained for days in the spring of 1889.

_____ The water levels began to rise in the river and the town.

_____ A man on horseback shouted a warning to the townspeople.

_____ A small dam on the river broke.

Number the events in order from 6 to 10.

_____ The flood piled debris 40 feet high at the railroad bridge.

_____ A wall of water more than 35 feet high crashed into the valley.

_____ When the rush of water was over, survivors were left clinging to the rooftops.

_____ Soon after the warning, the South Fork Dam gave way.

_____ The pile of debris caught fire.

Name _____ Date_____

Walls of Water
Chapter 2, "Rescue and Relief"

Mark each statement T for True or F for False.

_____ 1. The people of Johnstown cleaned up the flood without help.

_____ 2. The Red Cross had handled many major disasters before the Johnstown flood.

_____ 3. Clara Barton said the Red Cross would not help the people of Johnstown.

_____ 4. The flood victims needed food, shelter, and clothing.

_____ 5. More than 50 children were left without parents.

_____ 6. The stories told by flood survivors were full of tragedy and luck.

_____ 7. One man floated in the floodwaters for 17 hours.

_____ 8. People on a roof watched helplessly as others floated by.

_____ 9. One man floated on his house and landed in his office.

_____ 10. The floodwaters kept people away from the fire at the bridge.

Name _____ Date_____

Walls of Water
Chapter 3, "A Look Back at Johnstown"

Fill in the bubble beside the answer for each question.

1. Where is Johnstown located?

   Ⓐ on Lake Superior

   Ⓑ near the fork of three rivers

   Ⓒ on the coast of the Atlantic Ocean

2. Why was the South Fork Dam built?

   Ⓐ to irrigate crops in the nearby farms

   Ⓑ to keep boats off the river

   Ⓒ to make a lake to feed water to the canal

3. What job did many people in Johnstown have?

   Ⓐ They worked in steel mills.

   Ⓑ They raised crops on farms.

   Ⓒ They built railroad cars.

4. What did slag from the steel mills do?

   Ⓐ filled in the river channels and made the water move faster

   Ⓑ made good farmland along the river

   Ⓒ washed downstream from Johnstown

5. Who owned the land around the lake?

   Ⓐ mill workers

   Ⓑ the Fishing and Hunting Club

   Ⓒ both A and B

Name _____ Date_____

Walls of Water
Chapter 4, "The Great Flood of 1993"

Mark each statement T for True or F for False.

_____ 1. The Mississippi River runs from Minnesota to the Gulf of Mexico.

_____ 2. People have built locks, dams, and levees to keep the river

from overflowing.

_____ 3. People who live along the river get used to flooding now and then.

_____ 4. The melting of winter snow has little to do with spring flooding.

_____ 5. There was no flood warning for the people who lived along

the river.

Number the events in order from 1 to 5.

_____ Water ran off the land into rivers, raising the water levels.

_____ A dam broke, and the Great Flood of 1993 began.

_____ Heavy snow fell in the winter, and spring rains melted the snow.

_____ When a big storm hit in June of 1993, people got ready for a flood.

_____ The rain started in the fall of 1992, and the ground filled with water.

Name _____ Date_____

Walls of Water
Chapter 5, "After the Flood"

Mark each statement T for True or F for False.

_____ 1. In 1993, record rains fell in nine states.

_____ 2. City officials in the Mississippi River Basin were unprepared.

_____ 3. All the relief workers were unable to save lives, homes, or businesses.

_____ 4. Help came from all parts of the country.

_____ 5. More people died in the Great Flood of 1993 than in the Johnstown Flood of 1889.

Number the events in order from 1 to 5.

_____ Rescue workers meet immediate needs for food, drinking water, and medical care.

_____ Government workers and others help flood victims clean up, repair, rebuild, and replace.

_____ City officials and other groups prepare to help in case of flooding.

_____ Rain and flooding stop, and the rivers return to their banks.

_____ Service groups find temporary shelter for the flood victims.

Name _____ Date_____

Walls of Water
Chapter 6, "What Causes Floods?"

Fill in the bubble beside the answer for each question.

1. A sudden rush of swirling water is called

   Ⓐ a runoff.

   Ⓑ a flash flood.

   Ⓒ a 100-year flood.

2. Why does flooding cause more damage now than in previous times?

   Ⓐ Rivers were wider and could take more water.

   Ⓑ There were fewer people and businesses located in the

   floodplain then.

   Ⓒ both A and B

3. Most of the disaster aid the government gives out every year

   Ⓐ goes to other countries.

   Ⓑ goes to victims of forest fires.

   Ⓒ goes to flood victims.

4. What is another name for a tidal wave caused by underwater

   earthquakes?

   Ⓐ a tsunami

   Ⓑ a floodplain

   Ⓒ a 500-year flood

5. What rules have some states made to keep people safe from floods?

   Ⓐ Homes may not be rebuilt in flood zones.

   Ⓑ Wetlands must be kept dry.

   Ⓒ both A and B

Name _____ Date_____

Walls of Water
Think About It

Write about or give an oral presentation for each question.

1. How did steel mills make the Johnstown flood worse? _____

   _____

2. Foreshadowing is hinting at what will take place later in the story. Give

   an example of foreshadowing in the Johnstown flood chapters._____

   _____

   _____

3. Why do you think so many people help flood victims and other

   strangers in need? _____

   _____

4. Why are wetlands important? _____

   _____

Write About It

Choose one of the questions below. Write your answer on a sheet of paper.

1. Compare and contrast the Johnstown Flood and the Great Flood of 1993.
   How were the floods the same? How were they different?

2. The Red Cross helped the people of Johnstown. Write a report on how
   the Red Cross started and what the Red Cross does today.

3. Pretend you are a survivor of the Johnstown Flood. Write a story about
   what happened to you and your family.

Walls of Water

Chapter 1

*It kept raining. It rained all morning, and the water rose. Store owners	13
moved their goods to high shelves. At noon a small dam broke on the	27
Stony Creek River. It sent tons of lumber rolling down the river.	39
Many people stood by the banks of the river. They watched as the	52
logs tumbled through town. Still, the people of Johnstown did not worry.	64
They were used to flooding now and then.	72
It kept raining. The water rose higher. Some people had left their jobs	85
at noon. They went home to check on their families. A flood might keep	99
the family indoors. They would need drinking water and food. It might	111
take a few days for the storm to pass.*	120

Chapter 6

*Flooding is caused by lots of water that has nowhere to go. The water	14
can come from rain. Storms blow in from the ocean. They pour over	27
mountains. They drift across the land.	33
The water can also come from snow. A string of warm days will send	47
melted snow shooting down the mountains.	53
No matter where it comes from, the water has to go someplace. Some	66
of the water from rain and snow soaks into the soil. The rest runs off.	81
Runoff is greater where the land is steep. Water trickles down slick rock	94
faces and ice caps. It forms little creeks. The creeks flow into streams.	107
The streams flow into rivers. The rivers flow into bigger rivers. The	119
water* flows down the rivers and into the sea.	128

- The target rate for **Overcoming Adversity** is for students to read 120 words per minute correctly. The asterisks (*) mark 120 words.

- Listen to the student read the passage. Count the number of words read in one minute and the number of errors.

- For the reading rate, subtract the number of errors from the total number of words read.

- Have students enter scores on the Fluency Graph. See page 9.

Building Background

Name _____ Date _____

Walls of Water
What You Know

Write answers to these questions.

1. Name some natural disasters. **Ideas: floods, tornadoes, hurricanes, forest fires, blizzards, volcanoes, tidal waves, and ice storms**

2. What should you do when you hear a disaster warning? **Ideas: Move to a safe place; bring emergency supplies; get family together.**

3. What do some people do when they hear this kind of warning? **Ideas: Ignore it; go about their daily routine; watch television for updates.**

4. Choose a natural disaster, and explain how it can be prevented or controlled. **Ideas: Floods can be controlled with dams and levees; forest fires can be prevented by not allowing fires during droughts.**

There's a Word for It

Choose one of the words in the box to complete each sentence.

debris	levee	tsunami
disaster	tragedy	victims

1. A ___**tsunami**___ is a tidal wave.
2. The ___**debris**___ that the flood left behind littered the streets.
3. A serious misfortune or terrible event is a ___**tragedy**___.
4. The flood ___**victims**___ lost their homes.
5. We built a strong ___**levee**___ to hold back high water.
6. A tornado is a natural ___**disaster**___ that can destroy homes.

Overcoming Adversity • Book 5 — 63

Walls of Water

Chapter Quiz

Name _____ Date _____

Walls of Water
Chapter 1, "The Johnstown Flood, 1889"

Number the events in order from 1 to 5.

__4__ Tons of lumber rolled down the river.

__1__ It rained for days in the spring of 1889.

__2__ The water levels began to rise in the river and the town.

__5__ A man on horseback shouted a warning to the townspeople.

__3__ A small dam on the river broke.

Number the events in order from 6 to 10.

__8__ The flood piled debris 40 feet high at the railroad bridge.

__7__ A wall of water more than 35 feet high crashed into the valley.

__10__ When the rush of water was over, survivors were left clinging to the rooftops.

__6__ Soon after the warning, the South Fork Dam gave way.

__9__ The pile of debris caught fire.

Overcoming Adversity • Book 5 — 65

Walls of Water

Chapter Quiz

Name _____ Date _____

Walls of Water
Chapter 2, "Rescue and Relief"

Mark each statement T for True or F for False.

__F__ 1. The people of Johnstown cleaned up the flood without help.

__F__ 2. The Red Cross had handled many major disasters before the Johnstown flood.

__F__ 3. Clara Barton said the Red Cross would not help the people of Johnstown.

__T__ 4. The flood victims needed food, shelter, and clothing.

__T__ 5. More than 50 children were left without parents.

__T__ 6. The stories told by flood survivors were full of tragedy and luck.

__T__ 7. One man floated in the floodwaters for 17 hours.

__F__ 8. People on a roof watched helplessly as others floated by.

__T__ 9. One man floated on his house and landed in his office.

__F__ 10. The floodwaters kept people away from the fire at the bridge.

66 — Overcoming Adversity • Book 5

Walls of Water

Chapter Quiz

Name _____ Date _____

Walls of Water
Chapter 3, "A Look Back at Johnstown"

Fill in the bubble beside the answer for each question.

1. Where is Johnstown located?
   - Ⓐ on Lake Superior
   - ● near the fork of three rivers
   - Ⓒ on the coast of the Atlantic Ocean

2. Why was the South Fork Dam built?
   - Ⓐ to irrigate crops in the nearby farms
   - Ⓑ to keep boats off the river
   - ● to make a lake to feed water to the canal

3. What job did many people in Johnstown have?
   - ● They worked in steel mills.
   - Ⓑ They raised crops on farms.
   - Ⓒ They built railroad cars.

4. What did slag from the steel mills do?
   - ● filled in the river channels and made the water move faster
   - Ⓑ made good farmland along the river
   - Ⓒ washed downstream from Johnstown

5. Who owned the land around the lake?
   - Ⓐ mill workers
   - ● the Fishing and Hunting Club
   - Ⓒ both A and B

Overcoming Adversity • Book 5 — 67

Walls of Water

Answer Key

Chapter Quiz

Name _____ Date _____

Walls of Water
Chapter 4, "The Great Flood of 1993"

Mark each statement T for True or F for False.

_T_ 1. The Mississippi River runs from Minnesota to the Gulf of Mexico.

_T_ 2. People have built locks, dams, and levees to keep the river from overflowing.

_T_ 3. People who live along the river get used to flooding now and then.

_F_ 4. The melting of winter snow has little to do with spring flooding.

_F_ 5. There was no flood warning for the people who lived along the river.

Number the events in order from 1 to 5.

_3_ Water ran off the land into rivers, raising the water levels.

_5_ A dam broke, and the Great Flood of 1993 began.

_2_ Heavy snow fell in the winter, and spring rains melted the snow.

_4_ When a big storm hit in June of 1993, people got ready for a flood.

_1_ The rain started in the fall of 1992, and the ground filled with water.

68   Overcoming Adversity • Book 5

Walls of Water

Name _____ Date _____

Walls of Water
Chapter 5, "After the Flood"

Mark each statement T for True or F for False.

_T_ 1. In 1993, record rains fell in nine states.

_F_ 2. City officials in the Mississippi River Basin were unprepared.

_F_ 3. All the relief workers were unable to save lives, homes, or businesses.

_T_ 4. Help came from all parts of the country.

_F_ 5. More people died in the Great Flood of 1993 than in the Johnstown Flood of 1889.

Number the events in order from 1 to 5.

_2_ Rescue workers meet immediate needs for food, drinking water, and medical care.

_5_ Government workers and others help flood victims clean up, repair, rebuild, and replace.

_1_ City officials and other groups prepare to help in case of flooding.

_4_ Rain and flooding stop, and the rivers return to their banks.

_3_ Service groups find temporary shelter for the flood victims.

Overcoming Adversity • Book 5   69

Walls of Water

Chapter Quiz

Name _____ Date _____

Walls of Water
Chapter 6, "What Causes Floods?"

Fill in the bubble beside the answer for each question.

1. A sudden rush of swirling water is called
   - Ⓐ a runoff.
   - ● a flash flood.
   - Ⓒ a 100-year flood.

2. Why does flooding cause more damage now than in previous times?
   - Ⓐ Rivers were wider and could take more water.
   - Ⓑ There were fewer people and businesses located in the floodplain then.
   - ● both A and B

3. Most of the disaster aid the government gives out every year
   - Ⓐ goes to other countries.
   - Ⓑ goes to victims of forest fires.
   - ● goes to flood victims.

4. What is another name for a tidal wave caused by underwater earthquakes?
   - ● a tsunami
   - Ⓑ a floodplain
   - Ⓒ a 500-year flood

5. What rules have some states made to keep people safe from floods?
   - ● Homes may not be rebuilt in flood zones.
   - Ⓑ Wetlands must be kept dry.
   - Ⓒ both A and B

70   Overcoming Adversity • Book 5

Walls of Water

Name _____ Date _____

Walls of Water
Think About It

Write about or give an oral presentation for each question.

1. How did steel mills make the Johnstown flood worse? **Idea: Slag from the mills narrowed the channels and made the water move faster.**

2. Foreshadowing is hinting at what will take place later in the story. Give an example of foreshadowing in the Johnstown flood chapters. **Ideas: The South Fork Dam leaked; another dam broke; water was rising.**

3. Why do you think so many people help flood victims and other strangers in need? **Ideas: People realize they might need help in the future; people have skills that are needed.**

4. Why are wetlands important? **Ideas: Wetlands soak up lots of water; they help keep water from moving on and flooding towns.**

Write About It

Choose one of the questions below. Write your answer on a sheet of paper.

1. Compare and contrast the Johnstown Flood and the Great Flood of 1993. How were the floods the same? How were they different?

2. The Red Cross helped the people of Johnstown. Write a report on how the Red Cross started and what the Red Cross does today.

3. Pretend you are a survivor of the Johnstown Flood. Write a story about what happened to you and your family.

Overcoming Adversity • Book 5   71

Walls of Water

Name _____ Date_____

Robinson Crusoe's Adventures
What You Know

Write answers to these questions.

1. Did anyone ever give you advice you did not take but wished you had?

   What happened? _____

2. What are the most important things a person needs? _____

   _____

3. What kind of person would you want to have with you on a desert

   island? _____

   _____

4. What would you miss if you had been away from home for a while?____

   _____

There's a Word for It

Choose one of the words in the box to complete each sentence.

cannibal	capture	shelter
canoe	profit	spyglass

1. We paddled down the river in an old _____.

2. The man made a good _____ selling his goods.

3. A _____ prefers people to pork.

4. Another name for a small telescope is a _____.

5. The campers used a tent for _____.

6. It was hard to _____ the wild horse.

Word Lists

	Unfamiliar Words	Word Families	There's a Word for It	Proper Nouns
Chapter 1	bought merchant worse	England, English, Englishman promise, promised	profit	Africa London Yarmouth York
Chapter 2	advice among breath business divide fever grateful hurricane miracle plantation situation	survive, survived	capture, captors, captive shelter, sheltered	Brazil Xury (ZUR ree)
Chapter 3	candles daily dozen enjoyed explore finally knives progress routine wrote		spyglass	
Chapter 4	bored bury busy pistols taught umbrella	human, humans	cannibal canoe	Friday
Chapter 5	desperate drown evil known return sew spirits supplies urged	Spaniard, Spanish		
Chapter 6	governed mercy passenger prisoners			

Name _____ Date_____

Robinson Crusoe's Adventures
Chapter 1, "Going to Sea"

Number the events in order from 1 to 5.

_____ During a storm Crusoe gets seasick and promises never to sail again.

_____ Crusoe wants to become a sailor, but his family tries to talk him out of it.

_____ A nearby ship sends a rowboat to the rescue.

_____ Crusoe sails from London without telling his parents.

_____ When a second storm hits, the ship begins to sink.

Number the events in order from 6 to 10.

_____ On Crusoe's next trip pirates attack the ship and capture the crew.

_____ The people in Yarmouth are kind to the shipwrecked sailors.

_____ Pirates take Crusoe and the crew to a town in Africa and make them slaves.

_____ Crusoe sells African gold dust for a profit when he returns to England.

_____ Crusoe sails to Africa and learns how to be a good sailor.

Name _____ Date_____

Robinson Crusoe's Adventures
Chapter 2, "Stranded on an Island"

Mark each statement T for True or F for False.

_____ 1. Crusoe was afraid to escape.

_____ 2. The man who owned Crusoe sent him fishing.

_____ 3. Crusoe planned ahead and put supplies in the fishing boat.

_____ 4. While they were avoiding the pirates, Crusoe and Xury got lost.

_____ 5. A ship took Xury and Crusoe to England.

_____ 6. Crusoe refused to sell Xury.

_____ 7. The woman who was holding Crusoe's money had lost it.

_____ 8. Crusoe thought the sea was punishing him for being selfish.

_____ 9. Crusoe ended up alone on an island.

_____ 10. To stay safe Crusoe slept in a cave.

Name _____ **Date** _____

Robinson Crusoe's Adventures
Chapter 3, "Home Alone"

Mark each statement T for True or F for False.

_____ 1. Crusoe's ship had washed out to sea.

_____ 2. Crusoe was sad that everyone else had been lost.

_____ 3. Crusoe was not able to bring supplies from the ship.

_____ 4. One night the ship fell apart in a storm.

_____ 5. Crusoe's stay on the island began in September 1659.

_____ 6. Crusoe taught himself to build furniture and make useful things.

_____ 7. Crusoe built a fence around his camp to keep people out.

_____ 8. Crusoe liked to sleep late in the morning and hunt at midday.

_____ 9. After Crusoe got sick, he was afraid to explore the rest of the island.

_____ 10. Crusoe brought animals from the ship and caught animals on the island.

Name _____ **Date** _____

Robinson Crusoe's Adventures
Chapter 4, "A Footprint in the Sand"

Number the events in order from 1 to 5.

_____ Several years passed before Crusoe saw another footprint.

_____ Crusoe saw human bones on a part of the island where he had not been before.

_____ Crusoe had been alone on the island for 11 years.

_____ Crusoe stayed away from the part of the island where the bones were.

_____ One day Crusoe found a human footprint.

Number the events in order from 6 to 10.

_____ Through his spyglass Crusoe saw cannibals dancing around a fire.

_____ Crusoe called the man "Friday" and taught him English.

_____ The cannibals had two captives, but one man escaped from them.

_____ In his twenty-third year on the island, Crusoe saw smoke from a fire two miles away.

_____ When the cannibals came after the man, Crusoe shot them.

Name _____ Date_____

Robinson Crusoe's Adventures
Chapter 5, "Two Others Join Us"

Fill in the bubble beside the answer for each question.

1. After Crusoe learned about the white men on Friday's island, what did he plan to do?

   Ⓐ go to Friday's island

   Ⓑ go see the men who were there

   Ⓒ both A and B

2. What did Friday say they needed to get to the island?

   Ⓐ a lot of food

   Ⓑ a bigger boat

   Ⓒ both A and B

3. What kept Friday and Crusoe from starting their trip?

   Ⓐ wind

   Ⓑ hot sun

   Ⓒ rain

4. Whom did the cannibals capture?

   Ⓐ Friday's father

   Ⓑ Friday

   Ⓒ Friday's best friend

5. Why would the cannibals stay away from now on?

   Ⓐ They found other food.

   Ⓑ They were afraid of the guns.

   Ⓒ Their canoes were wrecked.

Name _____ Date_____

Robinson Crusoe's Adventures
Chapter 6, "Rescued"

Number the events in order from 1 to 5.

_____ Using a spyglass, Crusoe saw an English ship sailing toward him.

_____ The captain killed two sailors who were the ringleaders.

_____ Crusoe, Friday, the captain, and some sailors recaptured the ship.

_____ Sailors brought three captives ashore.

_____ When the sailors fell asleep, Friday and Crusoe set the captives free.

Number the events in order from 6 to 10.

_____ Crusoe moved back to Brazil.

_____ Friday and Crusoe sailed to England.

_____ In 1694 Crusoe visited the island.

_____ Crusoe found out his plantation in Brazil had done well.

_____ Friday stayed on the island when Crusoe left.

Name _____ Date _____

Robinson Crusoe's Adventures
Think About It

Write about or give an oral presentation for each question.

1. How did Crusoe feel when he saw the footprint in the sand? Why?_____

   _____

2. Crusoe talked about things he was not proud of doing. What were they?

   How did he feel about them later? _____

   _____

3. In the story Crusoe talks about buying and selling slaves. How is this

   attitude different from ours today? _____

   _____

4. Give some examples of foreshadowing from the story. _____

   _____

Write About It

Choose one of the questions below. Write your answer on a sheet of paper.

1. Robinson Crusoe was a survivor. What would you do to survive alone on an island? What would you do to keep from being bored?

2. Tell how this story fits the theme **Overcoming Adversity.** Give specific examples from the book.

3. Pretend that you are Robinson Crusoe. Write a journal entry about one day on the island.

4. Tell how this story fits the definition of an adventure story.

Robinson Crusoe's Adventures

Chapter 1

*At first I believed him. I said I would look into other ways of making	15
a living. That is what I did—for a while.	25
A year later I forgot my promise to my father. In September 1651, I set	40
off with a friend to London.	46
We sailed on his father's ship. I looked forward to a great adventure.	59
I left without a word to my parents. I did not think of their feelings at all.	76
I thought only about my own life.	83
I soon felt the sea was punishing me for my selfish ways. The ship was	98
tossed about in a hard storm. I was seasick and certain I would die. I	113
promised that if I ever got off* this ship, I would never get on another one.	129

Chapter 6

*Luckily for the captain, his captors had wandered into the forest and	12
had fallen asleep before they could carry out their plan.	22
Friday and I untied the men. We gave them guns and told them we	36
would help them take back control of the boat. First we had to do away	51
with the men on shore.	56
The captain killed the two ringleaders. The other sailors begged for	67
mercy and promised they would help us.	74
Meanwhile, Friday cleared out their boat. He took all the supplies, even	86
the sugar, which I had not tasted for years. I nearly cried when I saw it.	102
The captain said there were 26 men still on the ship. They knew they	116
would be hanged when* they returned to England.	124

- The target rate for **Overcoming Adversity** is for students to read 120 words per minute correctly. The asterisks (*) mark 120 words.

- Listen to the student read the passage. Count the number of words read in one minute and the number of errors.

- For the reading rate, subtract the number of errors from the total number of words read.

- Have students enter scores on the Fluency Graph. See page 9.

Name _____ Date _____

Robinson Crusoe's Adventures
What You Know

Write answers to these questions.

1. Did anyone ever give you advice you did not take but wished you had?
   What happened? **Answers will vary.**

2. What are the most important things a person needs? **Ideas: food,**
   shelter, clothing, companionship

3. What kind of person would you want to have with you on a desert
   island? **Ideas: someone with strong survival skills, someone**
   who is creative, or someone to talk to

4. What would you miss if you had been away from home for a while? ____
   Answers will vary.

There's a Word for It

Choose one of the words in the box to complete each sentence.

cannibal	capture	shelter
canoe	profit	spyglass

1. We paddled down the river in an old _____ **canoe** _____.
2. The man made a good _____ **profit** _____ selling his goods.
3. A _____ **cannibal** _____ prefers people to pork.
4. Another name for a small telescope is a _____ **spyglass** _____.
5. The campers used a tent for _____ **shelter** _____.
6. It was hard to _____ **capture** _____ the wild horse.

Overcoming Adversity • Book 6   75

Robinson Crusoe's Adventures

Name _____ Date _____

Robinson Crusoe's Adventures
Chapter 1, "Going to Sea"

Number the events in order from 1 to 5.

3 During a storm Crusoe gets seasick and promises never to sail again.

1 Crusoe wants to become a sailor, but his family tries to talk him out of it.

5 A nearby ship sends a rowboat to the rescue.

2 Crusoe sails from London without telling his parents.

4 When a second storm hits, the ship begins to sink.

Number the events in order from 6 to 10.

9 On Crusoe's next trip pirates attack the ship and capture the crew.

6 The people in Yarmouth are kind to the shipwrecked sailors.

10 Pirates take Crusoe and the crew to a town in Africa and make them slaves.

8 Crusoe sells African gold dust for a profit when he returns to England.

7 Crusoe sails to Africa and learns how to be a good sailor.

Overcoming Adversity • Book 6   77

Robinson Crusoe's Adventures

Name _____ Date _____

Robinson Crusoe's Adventures
Chapter 2, "Stranded on an Island"

Mark each statement T for True or F for False.

F 1. Crusoe was afraid to escape.

T 2. The man who owned Crusoe sent him fishing.

T 3. Crusoe planned ahead and put supplies in the fishing boat.

T 4. While they were avoiding the pirates, Crusoe and Xury got lost.

F 5. A ship took Xury and Crusoe to England.

F 6. Crusoe refused to sell Xury.

F 7. The woman who was holding Crusoe's money had lost it.

T 8. Crusoe thought the sea was punishing him for being selfish.

T 9. Crusoe ended up alone on an island.

F 10. To stay safe Crusoe slept in a cave.

78   Overcoming Adversity • Book 6

Robinson Crusoe's Adventures

Name _____ Date _____

Robinson Crusoe's Adventures
Chapter 3, "Home Alone"

Mark each statement T for True or F for False.

F 1. Crusoe's ship had washed out to sea.

T 2. Crusoe was sad that everyone else had been lost.

F 3. Crusoe was not able to bring supplies from the ship.

T 4. One night the ship fell apart in a storm.

T 5. Crusoe's stay on the island began in September 1659.

T 6. Crusoe taught himself to build furniture and make useful things.

F 7. Crusoe built a fence around his camp to keep people out.

F 8. Crusoe liked to sleep late in the morning and hunt at midday.

F 9. After Crusoe got sick, he was afraid to explore the rest of the island.

T 10. Crusoe brought animals from the ship and caught animals on the island.

Overcoming Adversity • Book 6   79

Robinson Crusoe's Adventures

Answer Key

Chapter Quiz

Name _____ Date _____

Robinson Crusoe's Adventures
Chapter 4, "A Footprint in the Sand"

Number the events in order from 1 to 5.

__3__ Several years passed before Crusoe saw another footprint.

__4__ Crusoe saw human bones on a part of the island where he had not been before.

__1__ Crusoe had been alone on the island for 11 years.

__5__ Crusoe stayed away from the part of the island where the bones were.

__2__ One day Crusoe found a human footprint.

Number the events in order from 6 to 10.

__7__ Through his spyglass Crusoe saw cannibals dancing around a fire.

__10__ Crusoe called the man "Friday" and taught him English.

__8__ The cannibals had two captives, but one man escaped from them.

__6__ In his twenty-third year on the island, Crusoe saw smoke from a fire two miles away.

__9__ When the cannibals came after the man, Crusoe shot them.

80   Overcoming Adversity • Book 6

Robinson Crusoe's Adventures

Chapter Quiz

Name _____ Date _____

Robinson Crusoe's Adventures
Chapter 5, "Two Others Join Us"

Fill in the bubble beside the answer for each question.

1. After Crusoe learned about the white men on Friday's island, what did he plan to do?
   - Ⓐ go to Friday's island
   - Ⓑ go see the men who were there
   - ● both A and B

2. What did Friday say they needed to get to the island?
   - Ⓐ a lot of food
   - ● a bigger boat
   - Ⓒ both A and B

3. What kept Friday and Crusoe from starting their trip?
   - Ⓐ wind
   - Ⓑ hot sun
   - ● rain

4. Whom did the cannibals capture?
   - ● Friday's father
   - Ⓑ Friday
   - Ⓒ Friday's best friend

5. Why would the cannibals stay away from now on?
   - Ⓐ They found other food.
   - ● They were afraid of the guns.
   - Ⓒ Their canoes were wrecked.

Overcoming Adversity • Book 6   81

Robinson Crusoe's Adventures

Chapter Quiz

Name _____ Date _____

Robinson Crusoe's Adventures
Chapter 6, "Rescued"

Number the events in order from 1 to 5.

__1__ Using a spyglass, Crusoe saw an English ship sailing toward him.

__4__ The captain killed two sailors who were the ringleaders.

__5__ Crusoe, Friday, the captain, and some sailors recaptured the ship.

__2__ Sailors brought three captives ashore.

__3__ When the sailors fell asleep, Friday and Crusoe set the captives free.

Number the events in order from 6 to 10.

__8__ Crusoe moved back to Brazil.

__6__ Friday and Crusoe sailed to England.

__9__ In 1694 Crusoe visited the island.

__7__ Crusoe found out his plantation in Brazil had done well.

__10__ Friday stayed on the island when Crusoe left.

82   Overcoming Adversity • Book 6

Robinson Crusoe's Adventures

Thinking and Writing

Name _____ Date _____

Robinson Crusoe's Adventures
Think About It

Write about or give an oral presentation for each question.

1. How did Crusoe feel when he saw the footprint in the sand? Why? _____
   Ideas: Crusoe was afraid; he was used to being alone.

2. Crusoe talked about things he was not proud of doing. What were they? How did he feel about them later? **Ideas: He lost touch with his family; he sold Xury; he tried to capture slaves; he seemed sorry later.**

3. In the story Crusoe talks about buying and selling slaves. How is this attitude different from ours today? **Ideas: We do not have slaves today; we do not think people should be bought or sold.**

4. Give some examples of foreshadowing from the story. **Idea: His parents warned him not to go to sea, and then he is shipwrecked.**

Write About It

Choose one of the questions below. Write your answer on a sheet of paper.

1. Robinson Crusoe was a survivor. What would you do to survive alone on an island? What would you do to keep from being bored?

2. Tell how this story fits the theme **Overcoming Adversity**. Give specific examples from the book.

3. Pretend that you are Robinson Crusoe. Write a journal entry about one day on the island.

4. Tell how this story fits the definition of an adventure story.

Overcoming Adversity • Book 6   83

Robinson Crusoe's Adventures

Name _____ Date_____

The Trojan War
What You Know

Write answers to these questions.

1. Why do you think wars start? _____

   _____

   _____

2. Would you rather be powerful, loved by others, or wise? Why?_____

   _____

3. What is a myth? _____

   _____

4. Many cultures have myths. Name a myth, and be ready to tell the story

   to the class._____

There's a Word for It

Choose one of the words in the box to complete each sentence.

archaeologists	prophecy	strife
oracle	shepherd	wisdom

1. In ancient times people asked an _____ for advice.

2. The _____ watched over the flock of sheep.

3. A simple misunderstanding turned into bitter _____.

4. _____ is made up of good sense and experience.

5. Scientists who study ancient ruins are called _____.

6. The oracle's _____ about the future was wrong.

Word Lists

	Unfamiliar Words	Word Families	There's a Word for It	Proper Nouns
Chapter 1	adored choose dare finally fought guests insulted marry meant noticed refuse ruined		prophecy strife wisdom	Aphrodite (af roh DEYE tee) Athena (uh THEE nah) Eris (EE ris) Greek Hera (HEER uh) King Peleus (PEA lee us) Mount Olympus (oh LIM pus) Thetis (THEE tis) Zeus (ZOOSE)
Chapter 2	bargain promise terrible	prince, princess Troy, Trojans	oracle shepherd	Achilles (ah KILL eez) Helen King Menelaus (men eh LAY us) Paris River Styx (STICKS) Sparta
Chapter 3	capture honored message reason supposed sword			Agamemnon (ag ah MEM non) Odysseus (oh DIS ee us)
Chapter 4	armor deserved retreated returned spear			Apollo (ah PAWL oh) Hector (HEK tor) Patroclus (pah TROH klus)
Chapter 5	coward death guide lose special statue tower			Sinon (SEYE non)
Chapter 6	awesome convinced danger directed magnificent scene thrilled		archaeologists (are key AH loh jists)	Cassandra (kah SAN drah)

Name _____ Date_____

The Trojan War
Chapter 1, "The Golden Apple"

Mark each statement T for True or F for False.

_____ **1.** The ancient Greek gods had many faults.

_____ **2.** Fortunately, the gods stayed on Mount Olympus away

from humans.

_____ **3.** Gods and goddesses could not fall in love with or marry humans.

_____ **4.** A prophecy said that Thetis's son would become greater than

his father.

_____ **5.** Thetis wanted to marry the young, handsome King Peleus.

Number the events in order from 1 to 5.

_____ Eris tossed a golden apple "for the fairest" to the guests.

_____ Thetis invited all the gods and goddesses except one to the wedding.

_____ Three goddesses argued over the apple.

_____ Thetis agreed to marry Peleus.

_____ Eris went to Thetis's wedding anyway.

Name _____ Date_____

The Trojan War
Chapter 2, "Paris Is the Judge"

Fill in the bubble beside the answer for each question.

1. What did the oracle say would happen to Achilles?

   Ⓐ He would die in battle.

   Ⓑ He would become a god.

   Ⓒ He would marry the most beautiful woman.

2. Which part of baby Achilles did not touch the River Styx?

   Ⓐ his heart

   Ⓑ his heel

   Ⓒ his hand

3. What did an oracle say would happen to Paris?

   Ⓐ He would become greater than his father.

   Ⓑ He would die in battle.

   Ⓒ He would cause Troy to burn.

4. What did Aphrodite promise Paris if he chose her?

   Ⓐ He would become a war hero.

   Ⓑ He would marry the most beautiful woman in the world.

   Ⓒ He would find more golden apples.

5. What did Aphrodite tell Paris?

   Ⓐ He was a prince.

   Ⓑ He was a shepherd.

   Ⓒ He was Zeus's son.

Overcoming Adversity • Book 7

Name _____ Date_____

The Trojan War
Chapter 3, "Love and War"

Mark each statement T for True or F for False.

_____ **1.** King Menelaus wanted to be on good terms with the Trojans.

_____ **2.** Paris did not think Helen was beautiful.

_____ **3.** King Menelaus could tell that Paris liked his wife.

_____ **4.** Aphrodite made Helen fall in love with Paris.

_____ **5.** Helen sent Paris away and stayed with King Menelaus.

_____ **6.** The king found out that Paris had stolen his wife and his treasure.

_____ **7.** All the Greek kings and heroes agreed to help King Menelaus.

_____ **8.** Odysseus pretended to be crazy to stay out of the war.

_____ **9.** Achilles hid from Odysseus by dressing up as a shepherd.

_____ **10.** Odysseus tricked Achilles into lifting the heavy sword.

Name _____ Date _____

The Trojan War
Chapter 4, "The Battles Rage"

Fill in the bubble beside the answer for each question.

1. Who was the leader of the Trojan army?

   Ⓐ Agamemnon

   Ⓑ Achilles

   Ⓒ Hector

2. How did the god Apollo fight against the Greeks?

   Ⓐ He sank their ships.

   Ⓑ He caused an illness.

   Ⓒ He melted their swords.

3. What did Achilles do when he got angry with Agamemnon?

   Ⓐ He took his army away.

   Ⓑ He sat in his tent and felt sorry for himself.

   Ⓒ both A and B

4. What made Achilles return to the war?

   Ⓐ His mother told him to fight.

   Ⓑ The Trojans killed his best friend.

   Ⓒ both A and B

5. Why could Achilles easily kill Hector?

   Ⓐ He knew the weak spot in the armor.

   Ⓑ He had a stronger sword than Hector.

   Ⓒ Apollo helped Achilles.

Name _____ Date_____

The Trojan War
Chapter 5, "The War Goes On"

Mark each statement T for True or F for False.

_____ 1. The Trojans wanted to kill Achilles because he had taken Helen.

_____ 2. Paris was brave but not handsome.

_____ 3. Apollo knew which part of Achilles' body could be hurt.

_____ 4. Paris killed Achilles by shooting him in the heart.

_____ 5. Odysseus wore Achilles' armor to honor him after Achilles died.

_____ 6. The Greeks did not know the gods were against them.

_____ 7. Odysseus stole the Trojans' armor to make them lose.

_____ 8. The Greeks hid the statue of Athena in their camp.

_____ 9. The Greeks boarded their ships and headed for home.

_____ 10. Odysseus came up with a plan to win the war.

Name _____ Date_____

The Trojan War
Chapter 6, "The Trojan Horse"

Number the events in order from 1 to 5.

_____ One man warned the Trojans, "Beware of Greeks bearing gifts!"

_____ The Greeks left the horse outside Troy and left.

_____ The Greeks built a huge wooden horse.

_____ Sinon told the Trojans the wooden horse was a gift.

_____ The Trojans came outside the city gates to sing and dance.

Number the events in order from 6 to 10.

_____ Aphrodite made Menelaus fall in love with Helen again.

_____ After the Trojans fell asleep, Greek soldiers climbed out of the horse.

_____ The prophecy came true because the Greeks burned Troy.

_____ The Greek soldiers killed all the Trojan men.

_____ The Trojans rolled the giant horse inside the city.

Name _____ Date_____

The Trojan War
Think About It

Write about or give an oral presentation for each question.

1. Today, who claims to predict the future? Do you think they can?_____

   _____

2. Paris chose beauty over wisdom and power. Do you agree with his

   choice? Why or why not? _____

   _____

3. What do you think would have happened if the Trojans had not taken

   the horse inside the city of Troy?_____

   _____

Write About It

Choose one of the questions below. Write your answer on a sheet of paper.

1. Each Greek god or goddess had special powers. Imagine that you are a
   Greek god. What power would you have? Why?

2. In an epic, the story is long, with lots of adventures, the heroes are
   larger than life, and the action takes place over a long time and in many
   places. Explain how this story is an epic.

3. Read more about the Greek gods and goddesses. Write a report about
   one who interests you.

4. The theme of this series is **Overcoming Adversity.** What kinds of
   adversity did the Greeks face? How did they overcome the adversity?

The Trojan War

Chapter 1

*Thetis was a beautiful sea goddess. She wanted to marry a handsome	12
god. She was insulted when a king named Peleus fell in love with her.	26
He was not a god. And he was not handsome.	36

Still, King Peleus loved Thetis with all his heart. He followed her	48
everywhere, except to Mount Olympus. Thetis did everything in her	58
power to get away from him. She had her eye on someone better.	71

Thetis was in love with Zeus, the most powerful god. Zeus had heard	84
a prophecy, which tells the future. The prophecy worried him very	95
much. It said that Thetis would give birth to a son who would become	109
greater than his father.	113

Zeus was very important. All the other* gods looked up to him.	125

Chapter 6

*The people were thrilled. They had not been beyond the city walls	12
for years. They streamed outside. They sang and danced. For the first	24
time in many years, they felt free.	31

Then they saw the huge wooden horse. Some were afraid of it. Others	44
thought it was a strange toy. Many wanted to pull it inside the city walls.	59

That's when Sinon stepped forward. "Greetings," he said. "I bring you	70
a gift."	72

Sinon explained that he was tired of the battle. He said he hated the	86
Greeks. He said Odysseus knew this. So Odysseus had left him behind	98
when the rest of the army sailed home.	106

Sinon said the Greeks had made the horse as an offering to Athena.	119
They* built the horse to thank her for her wisdom.	129

- The target rate for **Overcoming Adversity** is for students to read 120 words per minute correctly. The asterisks (*) mark 120 words.

- Listen to the student read the passage. Count the number of words read in one minute and the number of errors.

- For the reading rate, subtract the number of errors from the total number of words read.

- Have students enter scores on the Fluency Graph. See page 9.

Building Background

Name _____ **Date** _____

The Trojan War
What You Know

Write answers to these questions.

1. Why do you think wars start? **Ideas: Countries want control of something, such as water or land; one group takes something that belongs to another group.**

2. Would you rather be powerful, loved by others, or wise? Why? **Answers will vary.**

3. What is a myth? **Ideas: A story with some superhuman characters; it explains a belief or natural phenomenon; a popular belief.**

4. Many cultures have myths. Name a myth, and be ready to tell the story to the class. **Answers will vary.**

There's a Word for It

Choose one of the words in the box to complete each sentence.

| archaeologists | prophecy | strife |
| oracle | shepherd | wisdom |

1. In ancient times people asked an **oracle** for advice.
2. The **shepherd** watched over the flock of sheep.
3. A simple misunderstanding turned into bitter **strife**.
4. **Wisdom** is made up of good sense and experience.
5. Scientists who study ancient ruins are called **archaeologists**.
6. The oracle's **prophecy** about the future was wrong.

Overcoming Adversity • Book 7   87

The Trojan War

Chapter Quiz

Name _____ **Date** _____

The Trojan War
Chapter 1, "The Golden Apple"

Mark each statement T for True or F for False.

T 1. The ancient Greek gods had many faults.
F 2. Fortunately, the gods stayed on Mount Olympus away from humans.
F 3. Gods and goddesses could not fall in love with or marry humans.
T 4. A prophecy said that Thetis's son would become greater than his father.
F 5. Thetis wanted to marry the young, handsome King Peleus.

Number the events in order from 1 to 5.

4 Eris tossed a golden apple "for the fairest" to the guests.
2 Thetis invited all the gods and goddesses except one to the wedding.
5 Three goddesses argued over the apple.
1 Thetis agreed to marry Peleus.
3 Eris went to Thetis's wedding anyway.

Overcoming Adversity • Book 7   89

The Trojan War

Chapter Quiz

Name _____ **Date** _____

The Trojan War
Chapter 2, "Paris Is the Judge"

Fill in the bubble beside the answer for each question.

1. What did the oracle say would happen to Achilles?
● He would die in battle.
Ⓑ He would become a god.
Ⓒ He would marry the most beautiful woman.

2. Which part of baby Achilles did not touch the River Styx?
Ⓐ his heart
● his heel
Ⓒ his hand

3. What did an oracle say would happen to Paris?
Ⓐ He would become greater than his father.
Ⓑ He would die in battle.
● He would cause Troy to burn.

4. What did Aphrodite promise Paris if he chose her?
Ⓐ He would become a war hero.
● He would marry the most beautiful woman in the world.
Ⓒ He would find more golden apples.

5. What did Aphrodite tell Paris?
● He was a prince.
Ⓑ He was a shepherd.
Ⓒ He was Zeus's son.

90   Overcoming Adversity • Book 7

The Trojan War

Chapter Quiz

Name _____ **Date** _____

The Trojan War
Chapter 3, "Love and War"

Mark each statement T for True or F for False.

T 1. King Menelaus wanted to be on good terms with the Trojans.
F 2. Paris did not think Helen was beautiful.
F 3. King Menelaus could tell that Paris liked his wife.
T 4. Aphrodite made Helen fall in love with Paris.
F 5. Helen sent Paris away and stayed with King Menelaus.
T 6. The king found out that Paris had stolen his wife and his treasure.
F 7. All the Greek kings and heroes agreed to help King Menelaus.
T 8. Odysseus pretended to be crazy to stay out of the war.
F 9. Achilles hid from Odysseus by dressing up as shepherd.
T 10. Odysseus tricked Achilles into lifting the heavy sword.

Overcoming Adversity • Book 7   91

The Trojan War

Answer Key

Name _____ **Date** _____

The Trojan War
Chapter 4, "The Battles Rage"

Fill in the bubble beside the answer for each question.

1. Who was the leader of the Trojan army?
   - Ⓐ Agamemnon
   - Ⓑ Achilles
   - ● Hector

2. How did the god Apollo fight against the Greeks?
   - Ⓐ He sank their ships.
   - ● He caused an illness.
   - Ⓒ He melted their swords.

3. What did Achilles do when he got angry with Agamemnon?
   - Ⓐ He took his army away.
   - Ⓑ He sat in his tent and felt sorry for himself.
   - ● both A and B

4. What made Achilles return to the war?
   - Ⓐ His mother told him to fight.
   - ● The Trojans killed his best friend.
   - Ⓒ both A and B

5. Why could Achilles easily kill Hector?
   - ● He knew the weak spot in the armor.
   - Ⓑ He had a stronger sword than Hector.
   - Ⓒ Apollo helped Achilles.

92   Overcoming Adversity • Book 7

The Trojan War

Name _____ **Date** _____

The Trojan War
Chapter 5, "The War Goes On"

Mark each statement T for True or F for False.

- **F**   1. The Trojans wanted to kill Achilles because he had taken Helen.
- **F**   2. Paris was brave but not handsome.
- **T**   3. Apollo knew which part of Achilles' body could be hurt.
- **F**   4. Paris killed Achilles by shooting him in the heart.
- **T**   5. Odysseus wore Achilles' armor to honor him after Achilles died.
- **T**   6. The Greeks did not know the gods were against them.
- **F**   7. Odysseus stole the Trojans' armor to make them lose.
- **T**   8. The Greeks hid the statue of Athena in their camp.
- **F**   9. The Greeks boarded their ships and headed for home.
- **T**   10. Odysseus came up with a plan to win the war.

Overcoming Adversity • Book 7   93

The Trojan War

Name _____ **Date** _____

The Trojan War
Chapter 6, "The Trojan Horse"

Number the events in order from 1 to 5.

- **5**   One man warned the Trojans, "Beware of Greeks bearing gifts!"
- **2**   The Greeks left the horse outside Troy and left.
- **1**   The Greeks built a huge wooden horse.
- **4**   Sinon told the Trojans the wooden horse was a gift.
- **3**   The Trojans came outside the city gates to sing and dance.

Number the events in order from 6 to 10.

- **9**   Aphrodite made Menelaus fall in love with Helen again.
- **7**   After the Trojans fell asleep, Greek soldiers climbed out of the horse.
- **10**   The prophecy came true because the Greeks burned Troy.
- **8**   The Greek soldiers killed all the Trojan men.
- **6**   The Trojans rolled the giant horse inside the city.

94   Overcoming Adversity • Book 7

The Trojan War

Name _____ **Date** _____

The Trojan War
Think About It

Write about or give an oral presentation for each question.

1. Today, who claims to predict the future? Do you think they can? **Ideas: Astrologists or psychics; unlikely.**

2. Paris chose beauty over wisdom and power. Do you agree with his choice? Why or why not? **Ideas: No, love, intelligence, kindness, fairness, a sense of humor are all more important than beauty.**

3. What do you think would have happened if the Trojans had not taken the horse inside the city of Troy? **Ideas: The Greeks might not have won the war; Troy would not have burned.**

Write About It

Choose one of the questions below. Write your answer on a sheet of paper.

1. Each Greek god or goddess had special powers. Imagine that you are a Greek god. What power would you have? Why?

2. In an epic, the story is long, with lots of adventures, the heroes are larger than life, and the action takes place over a long time and in many places. Explain how this story is an epic.

3. Read more about the Greek gods and goddesses. Write a report about one who interests you.

4. The theme of this series is **Overcoming Adversity**. What kinds of adversity did the Greeks face? How did they overcome the adversity?

Overcoming Adversity • Book 7   95

The Trojan War

Name _____ Date_____

Monte Cristo's Prison Years
What You Know

Write answers to these questions.

1. What does it mean to be jealous? Why would someone be jealous of another person? _____

   _____

2. What is a trial? _____

   _____

3. What if you needed to dig a hole but had no shovel? What else could you use? _____

4. Were you ever blamed for something you did not do? How did you feel?

   _____

There's a Word for It

Choose one of the words in the box to complete each sentence.

abbot	dungeon	governor
bier	francs	traitor

1. Pierre spent his last few _____ to buy food.

2. Another word for *prison warden* is _____.

3. The _____ was a wise and respected man.

4. The prisoner was thrown into the dark _____.

5. He was a _____. He helped the enemy during the war.

6. The strong men put the coffin on the _____.

Word Lists

	Unfamiliar Words	Word Families	There's a Word for It	Proper Nouns
Chapter 1	accept fatal guards harbor	arrest, arrested comrade, comrades prison, prisoner, prisoners	governor	Count of Monte Cristo (MAHN tay KREES toh) Edmond Dantès (ed MAWN dahn TEHZ) France Frenchman Marseilles (mahr SAY) Mercédès (mehr say DEHZ) Villefort (veel FAWR)
Chapter 2	continued government impossible swollen		abbot dungeon francs	
Chapter 3	courage dangerous innocent inspector refuse treasure trial violent		traitor	Abbot Faria (FAH ree ah) Toulouse (too LOOZE)
Chapter 4	betray continual doubt			Napoleon (nah poh lay OWN)
Chapter 5	drew heir strength			Italy Spada (SPAH dah)
Chapter 6		remain, remained	bier (BEERH)	

Name _____ Date_____

Monte Cristo's Prison Years
Chapter 1, "The Prison"

Mark each statement T for True or F for False.

____ 1. At first Dantès did not know where the guards were taking him.

____ 2. Dantès was chained to the boat.

____ 3. Dantès thought the letter had proof against him.

____ 4. Dantès trusted Villefort because he burned the letter.

____ 5. Dantès was not loyal to France.

____ 6. Dantès had committed a crime.

____ 7. The boat was headed toward a prison.

____ 8. Dantès promised not to escape and kept his promise.

____ 9. Everything was clear to Dantès as he climbed the steps to the prison.

____ 10. Dantès was given bread and water for dinner and fresh straw for a bed.

Name _____ Date_____

Monte Cristo's Prison Years
Chapter 2, "A Worse Place"

Fill in the bubble beside the answer for each question.

1. How did Dantès spend his first night in prison?

   Ⓐ trying to escape

   Ⓑ standing and weeping

   Ⓒ sleeping soundly

2. What did Dantès want?

   Ⓐ to see the prison governor

   Ⓑ to eat better food

   Ⓒ to move to a new cell

3. What happened to the abbot who had Dantès' cell before him?

   Ⓐ He died.

   Ⓑ He went mad.

   Ⓒ He was set free.

4. What did Dantès ask the jailer to do for him?

   Ⓐ help him escape

   Ⓑ take a note to Mercédès

   Ⓒ get him a better cell

5. Where was Dantès taken after he threatens the jailer?

   Ⓐ to be tortured

   Ⓑ to the dungeon

   Ⓒ to the governor

Name _____ Date_____

Monte Cristo's Prison Years
Chapter 3, "The Two Prisoners"

Mark each statement T for True or F for False.

_____ 1. A year passed before the inspector visited the prison.

_____ 2. The prisoners told the inspector that the food was fine.

_____ 3. The inspector cared about how the prisoners were treated.

_____ 4. The inspector visited Dantès in the dungeon.

_____ 5. Dantès begged to be shot if he were guilty of a crime.

_____ 6. The inspector thought seventeen months in prison was not very long.

_____ 7. Dantès believed that Villefort was very kind to him.

_____ 8. The Abbot Faria refused to share his treasure with the government.

_____ 9. Dantès' records showed that he was innocent.

_____ 10. The inspector arranged a trial for Dantès.

Name _____ Date _____

Monte Cristo's Prison Years
Chapter 4, "Number 34 and Number 27"

Fill in the bubble beside the answer for each question.

1. What did Dantès decide to do after four years in prison?

   Ⓐ dig a tunnel to the sea

   Ⓑ starve himself

   Ⓒ write letters to the newspapers

2. Dantès heard something in the middle of the night. What was it?

   Ⓐ a scratching sound

   Ⓑ a crying prisoner

   Ⓒ dripping water

3. What did Dantès decide to do with the other prisoner?

   Ⓐ kill him

   Ⓑ stop him from digging

   Ⓒ help him dig

4. What did Dantès dig with?

   Ⓐ a dinner fork

   Ⓑ a pan handle

   Ⓒ the jailer's sword

5. How did the other prisoner plan to escape?

   Ⓐ go over the wall

   Ⓑ steal keys from a guard

   Ⓒ swim to an island

Name _____ Date _____

Monte Cristo's Prison Years
Chapter 5, "The Treasure"

Mark each statement T for True or F for False.

_____ 1. Dantès and Faria met at night and planned their escape from prison.

_____ 2. Dantès taught Faria history and several languages.

_____ 3. Faria helped Dantès figure out who was to blame for putting him in prison.

_____ 4. Dantès decides to leave Faria behind because he is too sick to escape.

_____ 5. Faria told Dantès about a treasure.

_____ 6. Faria stole the money from the Spada family.

_____ 7. The Count of Spada had left his money to Faria.

_____ 8. Dantès wanted the money for himself.

_____ 9. Until he became ill, Faria did not plan to tell Dantès about the treasure.

_____ 10. Faria thought of Dantès as his son.

Name _____ **Date**_____

Monte Cristo's Prison Years
Chapter 6, "Escape"

Number the events in order from 1 to 5.

_____ The guards put Faria's body in a canvas sack.

_____ Faria told Dantès not to call for help even though he was dying.

_____ The turnkey found Faria dead and called for help.

_____ Dantès heard someone calling him from Faria's dungeon.

_____ Before he died, Faria told Dantès to hurry to Monte Cristo.

Number the events in order from 6 to 10.

_____ Dantès got into the sack and sewed up the sack from the inside.

_____ The men tied a weight to the sack and swung it to and fro.

_____ Instead of burying the body, the men threw it into the sea.

_____ Dantès took Faria's body out of the sack and moved it to his cell.

_____ The men carried the sack outside the prison.

Name _____ Date_____

Monte Cristo's Prison Years
Think About It

Write about or give an oral presentation for each question.

1. How do you think his years in prison have changed Dantès? _____

_____

2. Irony is the opposite of the expected outcome. Give some examples of
   irony from the story. _____

_____

3. What do you think Dantès will do when he gets out of the sack?_____

_____

Write About It

Choose one of the questions below. Write your answer on a sheet of paper.

1. The theme for these books is **Overcoming Adversity.** How did Dantès
   react at first? Who helped him to overcome adversity?

2. Pretend you are Dantès. Write a letter to Mercédès, telling her about life
   in the dungeon.

3. One element of this story is suspense. At the end of the story, things
   look hopeless for Dantès. But the introduction says Dantès becomes the
   Count of Monte Cristo. Write your own ending for this story.

4. Find three examples of irony in the story. Describe and explain the
   irony in each situation.

Monte Cristo's Prison Years

Chapter 1

*Dantès turned and saw that they had got out to sea. He turned to the	15
nearest guard. "Comrade," said he, "I beg you to tell me where we are	29
going. I am Captain Dantès, a loyal Frenchman. Tell me where you are	42
taking me. I promise you on my honor I will accept my fate."	55
Then the guard asked, "You are from Marseilles and a sailor, and yet	68
you do not know where you are going?"	76
"On my honor, I have no idea."	83
"Unless you cannot see, or have never been outside the harbor, you	95
must know."	97
"I do not."	100
"Look round you." Dantès rose and looked forward. Then he saw the	112
black and frowning rock on which stands the* prison.	121

Chapter 6

*Dantès could only clasp his hands and cry, "Oh, my friend, my	12
friend, do not speak this way!"	18
"There is no hope," answered Faria, shaking his head. "Now lift me	30
on my bed, for I can no longer support myself."	40
Dantès took the old man in his arms and placed him on the bed.	54
"And now, my dear friend," said Faria, "I wish you happiness and	66
riches. My son, I bless you!" The young man fell on his knees, leaning	80
his head against the old man's bed.	87
"Listen, now, to what I say. There really is a treasure. If you do escape,	102
remember that the poor abbot, whom all the world called mad, was	114
not so. Hurry to Monte Cristo.*	120

- The target rate for **Overcoming Adversity** is for students to read 120 words per minute correctly. The asterisks (*) mark 120 words.

- Listen to the student read the passage. Count the number of words read in one minute and the number of errors.

- For the reading rate, subtract the number of errors from the total number of words read.

- Have students enter scores on the Fluency Graph. See page 9.

Answer Key

Building Background

Name _____ **Date** _____

Monte Cristo's Prison Years
What You Know

Write answers to these questions.

1. What does it mean to be jealous? Why would someone be jealous of another person? **Idea: To be jealous is to want something that someone else has—looks, talents, friends, or money.**

2. What is a trial? **A trial is a court hearing held to decide if a person accused of a crime is innocent or guilty.**

3. What if you needed to dig a hole but had no shovel? What else could you use? **Ideas: hands, spoon, or knife**

4. Were you ever blamed for something you did not do? How did you feel? **Ideas: angry, wanted revenge; asked for help; found proof**

There's a Word for It

Choose one of the words in the box to complete each sentence.

| abbot | dungeon | governor |
| bier | francs | traitor |

1. Pierre spent his last few ____**francs**____ to buy food.
2. Another word for *prison warden* is ____**governor**____
3. The ____**abbot**____ was a wise and respected man.
4. The prisoner was thrown into the dark ____**dungeon**____
5. He was a ____**traitor**____. He helped the enemy during the war.
6. The strong men put the coffin on the ____**bier**____.

Overcoming Adversity • Book 8   99

Monte Cristo's Prison Years

Chapter Quiz

Name _____ **Date** _____

Monte Cristo's Prison Years
Chapter 1, "The Prison"

Mark each statement T for True or F for False.

T 1. At first Dantès did not know where the guards were taking him.

F 2. Dantès was chained to the boat.

T 3. Dantès thought the letter had proof against him.

T 4. Dantès trusted Villefort because he burned the letter.

F 5. Dantès was not loyal to France.

F 6. Dantès had committed a crime.

T 7. The boat was headed toward a prison.

F 8. Dantès promised not to escape and kept his promise.

F 9. Everything was clear to Dantès as he climbed the steps to the prison.

T 10. Dantès was given bread and water for dinner and fresh straw for a bed.

Overcoming Adversity • Book 8   101

Monte Cristo's Prison Years

Chapter Quiz

Name _____ **Date** _____

Monte Cristo's Prison Years
Chapter 2, "A Worse Place"

Fill in the bubble beside the answer for each question.

1. How did Dantès spend his first night in prison?
   - Ⓐ trying to escape
   - ● standing and weeping
   - Ⓒ sleeping soundly

2. What did Dantès want?
   - ● to see the prison governor
   - Ⓑ to eat better food
   - Ⓒ to move to a new cell

3. What happened to the abbot who had Dantès' cell before him?
   - Ⓐ He died.
   - ● He went mad.
   - Ⓒ He was set free.

4. What did Dantès ask the jailer to do for him?
   - Ⓐ help him escape
   - ● take a note to Mercédès
   - Ⓒ get him a better cell

5. Where was Dantès taken after he threatens the jailer?
   - Ⓐ to be tortured
   - ● to the dungeon
   - Ⓒ to the governor

102   Overcoming Adversity • Book 8

Monte Cristo's Prison Years

Chapter Quiz

Name _____ **Date** _____

Monte Cristo's Prison Years
Chapter 3, "The Two Prisoners"

Mark each statement T for True or F for False.

T 1. A year passed before the inspector visited the prison.

F 2. The prisoners told the inspector that the food was fine.

F 3. The inspector cared about how the prisoners were treated.

T 4. The inspector visited Dantès in the dungeon.

T 5. Dantès begged to be shot if he were guilty of a crime.

T 6. The inspector thought seventeen months in prison was not very long.

T 7. Dantès believed that Villefort was very kind to him.

F 8. The Abbot Faria refused to share his treasure with the government.

F 9. Dantès' records showed that he was innocent.

F 10. The inspector arranged a trial for Dantès.

Overcoming Adversity • Book 8   103

Monte Cristo's Prison Years

Overcoming Adversity • Book 8   **109**

Answer Key

Monte Cristo's Prison Years

Chapter Quiz

Name _____ Date _____

Monte Cristo's Prison Years
Chapter 4, "Number 34 and Number 27"

Fill in the bubble beside the answer for each question.

1. What did Dantès decide to do after four years in prison?
   Ⓐ dig a tunnel to the sea
   ● starve himself
   Ⓒ write letters to the newspapers

2. Dantès heard something in the middle of the night. What was it?
   ● a scratching sound
   Ⓑ a crying prisoner
   Ⓒ dripping water

3. What did Dantès decide to do with the other prisoner?
   Ⓐ kill him
   Ⓑ stop him from digging
   ● help him dig

4. What did Dantès dig with?
   Ⓐ a dinner fork
   ● a pan handle
   Ⓒ the jailer's sword

5. How did the other prisoner plan to escape?
   Ⓐ go over the wall
   Ⓑ steal keys from a guard
   ● swim to an island

104   Overcoming Adversity • Book 8

Monte Cristo's Prison Years

Chapter Quiz

Name _____ Date _____

Monte Cristo's Prison Years
Chapter 5, "The Treasure"

Mark each statement T for True or F for False.

_T_ 1. Dantès and Faria met at night and planned their escape from prison.

_F_ 2. Dantès taught Faria history and several languages.

_T_ 3. Faria helped Dantès figure out who was to blame for putting him in prison.

_F_ 4. Dantès decides to leave Faria behind because he is too sick to escape.

_T_ 5. Faria told Dantès about a treasure.

_F_ 6. Faria stole the money from the Spada family.

_T_ 7. The Count of Spada had left his money to Faria.

_F_ 8. Dantès wanted the money for himself.

_F_ 9. Until he became ill, Faria did not plan to tell Dantès about the treasure.

_T_ 10. Faria thought of Dantès as his son.

Overcoming Adversity • Book 8   105

Monte Cristo's Prison Years

Chapter Quiz

Name _____ Date _____

Monte Cristo's Prison Years
Chapter 6, "Escape"

Number the events in order from 1 to 5.

_5_ The guards put Faria's body in a canvas sack.

_2_ Faria told Dantès not to call for help even though he was dying.

_4_ The turnkey found Faria dead and called for help.

_1_ Dantès heard someone calling him from Faria's dungeon.

_3_ Before he died, Faria told Dantès to hurry to Monte Cristo.

Number the events in order from 6 to 10.

_7_ Dantès got into the sack and sewed up the sack from the inside.

_9_ The men tied a weight to the sack and swung it to and fro.

_10_ Instead of burying the body, the men threw it into the sea.

_6_ Dantès took Faria's body out of the sack and moved it to his cell.

_8_ The men carried the sack outside the prison.

106   Overcoming Adversity • Book 8

Monte Cristo's Prison Years

Thinking and Writing

Name _____ Date _____

Monte Cristo's Prison Years
Think About It

Write about or give an oral presentation for each question.

1. How do you think his years in prison have changed Dantès? **Ideas: Dantès learned a lot from Faria; he will not be as trusting as he was before.**

2. Irony is the opposite of the expected outcome. Give some examples of irony from the story. **Ideas: Dantès tells the inspector to believe what Villefort wrote; Dantès prepares to be buried, not drowned.**

3. What do you think Dantès will do when he gets out of the sack? **Ideas: He will go to Monte Cristo to get the treasure; he will get revenge.**

Write About It

Choose one of the questions below. Write your answer on a sheet of paper.

1. The theme for these books is **Overcoming Adversity**. How did Dantès react at first? Who helped him to overcome adversity?

2. Pretend you are Dantès. Write a letter to Mercédès, telling her about life in the dungeon.

3. One element of this story is suspense. At the end of the story, things look hopeless for Dantès. But the introduction says Dantès becomes the Count of Monte Cristo. Write your own ending for this story.

4. Find three examples of irony in the story. Describe and explain the irony in each situation.

Overcoming Adversity • Book 8   107

Monte Cristo's Prison Years